The

Couple's

Guide

to the

Best

<u>Erotic</u>

Videos

Steve and Elizabeth Brent

The Couple's Guide to the Best *Erotic* Videos

 St. Martin's Griffen ❧ New York

THE COUPLE'S GUIDE TO THE BEST EROTIC VIDEOS. Copyright
© 1997 by Adult Video Enterprise. All rights reserved.
Printed in the United States of America. No part of this
book may be used or reproduced in any manner whatso-
ever without written permission except in the case of brief
quotations embodied in critical articles or reviews. For information, address St. Martin's Press, 175 Fifth Avenue,
New York, N.Y. 10010.

Library of Congress Cataloging-in-Publication Data

Brent, Steve.
    The couple's guide to the best erotic videos / Steve
and Elizabeth Brent—1st ed.
        p. cm.
    ISBN 0-312-15081-4
    1. Erotic films—History and criticism. 2. Erotic
films—Plots, themes, etc. 3. Erotic films—Catalogs.
    I. Brent, Elizabeth.
    II. Title.
PN1995.9.S45B68 1997
791.43'6538—dc20   96-45960
                                                        CIP

First St. Martin's Griffin Edition: April 1997

10 9 8 7 6 5 4 3 2 1

Books are available in quantity for promotional or pre-
mium use. Write to Director of Special Sales, St. Martin's
Press, 175 Fifth Avenue, New York, NY 10010, for information on discounts and terms, or call toll-free (800) 221-
7945. In New York, call (212) 674-5151 (ext. 645).

contents

Part One

Part One

Views

Chapter 1

Looking for Love

*F*antasy: You are alone with an attractive stranger. A business trip, perhaps, far away from home, far away from everyday responsibilities and obligations. You're having a drink together in your hotel room. You quietly take a pillbox from your suitcase and remove a small pink capsule. You slip it into the stranger's drink. The pill is an amazing substance that quickly transforms the other person into an all-consuming, lust-addled Sex God. You tear off your clothes and make wild love all night long.

Yes, I know, it's a simple, bare-bones generic type of fantasy. Not a feather boa, whip, vibrator, or silk negligee in sight—but hasn't everyone, at some time in their lives, secretly wished that they possessed a genuine, effective aphrodisiac? I'm not talking about a miracle pill for the sexually dysfunctional or even an illicit drug to snare unsuspecting love partners, but a stimulator of pleasure, an enhancer and intensifier of the act—for both men and women.

The list of foods with supposed aphrodisiac qualities is well known: asparagus, caviar, oysters, lobster, chocolate, and other, more bizarre substances, like tiger penis and rhino horn. And what male hasn't heard whispered tales of the infamous Spanish

Fly—cantharis powder—which, when slipped into food or drink, supposedly drives women wild with desire?

Unfortunately, the general consensus is that aphrodisiacs don't work and some are even dangerous. So far, the search for a sure-fire love potion has been a failure.

Until now.

Now there's an aphrodisiac that is cheap, readily available, and extremely effective. You don't need a doctor's prescription and it doesn't involve pills or injections. You might not be able to slip it into a stranger's drink, but with some creative planning it can be used just as productively as our fantasy substance.

It's inexpensive and fun.

And it works.

Here's the new fantasy: It's Saturday night and you're home with your spouse or partner or just hanging around with a special friend. The kids are in bed—maybe there aren't any kids. At any rate, you've got nothing planned. "How about a movie?" one of you says. You're elected to pick up the tape.

You're cruising the shelves at the local mom-and-pop video store. Pretty much empty. Well, it's Saturday night, what did you expect? The folks who came in during the day got all the new releases.

But . . .

In the back of the store there's that special section that's blocked off from the main room. As much out of curiosity as anything else, you push through the doors. There you are, surrounded by hundreds of video boxes, all showing beautiful people, most of them naked. It looks good to you. Suddenly you've got an idea: Why not rent one of these films and just see what it's all about? Who knows, maybe it could lead to something interesting later in the evening.

So you do. You get lucky and you pick out a good one. It works. The evening turns out to be *very* interesting.

This fantasy is a lot more believable than the first one. I know because it happened to me, not exactly this way, but the effect was the same.

Trust me on this. Man or woman, friend, live-in, mate, or

lover—forget asparagus and oysters: Rent an erotic videotape. Unfolding in front of you, you'll find a fantasy world populated by handsome men and lovely women performing the most beautiful, exciting, intimate acts for your pleasure.

Prepare to unleash your erotic imagination.

Chapter 2

The Forbidden Zone

*W*hy Steve and Elizabeth Brent? What makes us experts in erotica?

We're not, and that's exactly the point.

Beth and I are an average couple living in a smallish town 45 minutes outside New York City. We have two children, a twelve-year-old son, and a daughter who is six. Both of them attend public school. Our house is a sort-of colonial with a large yard. We have lots of flowers, trees, and a vegetable garden.

Beth works as a nursing supervisor, and I'm a freelance writer who usually does technical assignments in the field of medicine. I'm also a part-time novelist.

Several years ago, I was writing a mystery novel when I decided to make a large element of the plot hinge on an X-rated video that the hero rents at his local video store (don't bother looking for the book, it was never sold). At the time, I knew very little about X-rated tapes except that my local video store carried a large supply in a small room off the main area. I knew what they were, of course, but I had never rented one—not out of moral censure or prudery, I'm as sexually liberated as the next person—but primarily out of embarrassment. Besides, I was sure my wife would not be interested.

But the more I thought about it, the more I realized that *I* was interested. The work on my novel offered a perfect excuse: research—it came with the job. It also supplied enough incentive and encouragement to make me overcome my initial embarrassment at renting one of *those* tapes.

Beth had collected the kids and gone off to her sister's for a week to give me time to work on my book. As soon as the Volvo station wagon disappeared around the corner, I hustled down to the video store to begin my research. I wasted some time wandering around the main room, checking to see that no one I knew was in the store, then ducked through the batwing doors into what I had begun to think of as The Forbidden Zone. There, I found myself all alone in a whole new world.

There were hundreds of tapes, and as far as I could see there was very little to distinguish one from another. They all had naked women on the covers of the boxes, sometimes there were naked guys as well. All of these naked people were engaged in different sorts of serious sexual activity, or looking as though they were *about* to engage in different sorts of serious sexual activity. Almost all of the people in the pictures would be characterized, I believe, as being at least good-looking and, in many cases, beautiful. The titles were pretty much uniformly stupid, either jokey takeoffs like *Screw the Right Thing*, or overtly raunchy like *Up and Cummers*.

Fairly confused, and generally unsure, I decided that I had no real basis for making any sort of rational decision. I didn't even know if a rational decision was possible. So I grabbed a couple of tapes off the shelf at random and went back out to the cashier.

My heart sank when I saw the checkout lady—a matronly woman about the same age and physical description as my own mother. But this was *work*, I reminded myself. I had an excuse! Of course the lady rented me the videos without a hint of disapproval or even interest, and I was soon back home, alone with my TV set and my trusty VCR.

I was lucky. The tapes I rented weren't bad. They were exciting. I watched both of them, soon learning that the fast-forward function on the remote is an indispensable tool for watching a sex movie. Especially when viewing alone.

Over the next week I watched around ten tapes and even found time to work on my novel. Some of the tapes were terrible, stupid beyond belief, offensive, a real turnoff. But some were just as good as the first ones I had rented. A few of them were even better. The people were beautiful, the sex was athletic and interesting, no one looked as if they were on drugs or being coerced in any way, and they sure were a turn-on.

After the week away, my wife returned home. She was surprised at my even-warmer-than-usual welcome.

The weekend rolled around and I rented one of the better videos I had already seen. I told my wife what I was up to. After the kids went to bed, I locked the bedroom door and rolled the tape.

Surprise, surprise. Beth found it pretty darn interesting. That night we burned up the bed like we hadn't done in quite some time.

Since then I've watched many of these tapes. Some of them had to do with writing my novel, but that particular book has been finished for quite some time now. I've seen a lot of good erotic videos, and the effect has remained the same. When you watch good-looking people making love, the effect is combustible. Put in a tape, lie back, and wait to catch fire.

But I've also wasted a lot of time, and money, on bad tapes. What I needed was a guide. Not one that simply lists the films and gives a couple of lines of synopsis—they already have these. Nor a guide written by some guy who indiscriminately loves the entire genre—these exist as well. But a guide for a regular man or woman who rents the occasional adult video for recreational purposes, and who would like to skip the really bad ones. I looked around and found that there weren't any such guides.

So I wrote one myself, the one you're now reading. I did the research, read reviews, and watched tapes. I asked my wife, Beth, to watch them with me and give me her opinion along the way. I wanted to know what she liked, and why. Her thoughts were important because I wanted this book to be for couples: men and women together. When I wasn't sure about a video, a performer, or a situation, I did what I usually do in life: I asked Beth. Her opinions are in the reviews right along with, and equal to, mine.

Along the way I learned a lot about the world of erotic videos: the directors, the stars, how they make them, what they cost, the problems of production, and much, much more. All of which I found fascinating and fun, and which I felt other people would find entertaining as well. But primarily I figured out how, the great majority of the time, not to get stuck with bad tapes. Believe me, my wife appreciates this skill. And so, I hope, will you.

How did we go about the research? Most of the tapes were rented at our local mom-and-pop video store. At first I thought I would study sex magazines and write to distributors everywhere to get tapes. But then I decided that wouldn't replicate the experience of most of the people we wanted to reach. In the end I tried to find as many convenient sources as possible because there are whole states where it's illegal to sell these tapes, though it's perfectly legal to buy them through the mail. But I wanted to limit the pool of possibilities to those tapes that can be found easily.

So, for all the friendly counterpersons down at my local video store, All World Video, I want to let you know that I am not a strange sex fiend who has to see hundreds of XXX videos to maintain his sex life. I was writing a book. Really.

As I said at the beginning of this chapter, Beth and I are not experts in the field of erotica. We're just a normal couple interested in enhancing our sexual pleasure. There are *lots* of people out there who know a great deal about eroticism, filmmaking, and the business of both. Many people have whole careers in the field. But now that this book is finished, we can't wait to get back to our old schedule of an erotic tape every once in a while, slotted in between all the mainstream tapes we missed out on because we were busy with research. Surprisingly, we're not burned out on erotica. Even after seeing a ton of tapes, they still retain their power to turn us on.

We feel these tapes are special. Making love is not something most of us do every day, especially those of us who have kids. When we do make love, we like for it to be pleasurable and, if not unique, at least not completely predictable. Sometimes it's lights on, sometimes it's lights off, sometimes with tapes, sometimes without. Variety, the spice of a good sex life.

Chapter 3

Forget Hollywood

P eople see a lot of regular in-the-theater movies simply because they've heard they're sexy. Did people flock to see *Basic Instinct* because it is an intriguing murder mystery? No, most viewers went to see it because they knew that Sharon Stone and Michael Douglas spent time in bed together and they would get to see a lot of flesh. To say nothing of Sharon Stone's quick, cross-the-legs pubic flash.

I saw the movie and had to laugh. I could have taken everyone in the audience down to the local video store and rented any number of films that featured women a lot better looking and better built than Sharon Stone and men who were a *whole* lot better looking and better built than Michael Douglas. And the people in the video would engage in *real* sex, where you could see them do everything. As opposed to the Hollywood version, where you have to feed your fantasies with guesswork and glimpses.

Sex. This is what people want to see. That's why they went to *Basic Instinct*, *Fatal Attraction*, *Indecent Exposure*. And why Hollywood sunk its money into the execrable *Showgirls* and *Jade* and scores of other sensationalist films. But what the audience got was a distant second best.

Why don't people go rent an erotic video? Many people do,

but I believe most don't because, primarily, they are embarrassed. People will quickly give you many different reasons why they don't want to rent erotic films, but when questioned further it almost always comes back to the same few elements: fear, shame, embarrassment, not wanting to look foolish, and being afraid of ridicule and rejection from their partner.

These are real reasons, and I understand that.

But, let me put it this way. Almost everyone in the world is interested in and desires sex. Almost everyone is excited by seeing other people have sex. A recent scientific experiment showed erotic tapes to groups of men and women, all of whom were wired up to machines that measured heart rate, temperature, perspiration, and other indicators of sexual arousal.

In the interviews after watching, the men admitted to being turned on by the tapes. Almost all the women said that they were not turned on. But the measurements showed that all the men, *and all the women*, were sexually excited to the same degree. None was unaffected, yet the women felt they couldn't admit to finding pleasure, or even responding, to the films.

There is no reason for adults to deny themselves the pleasure of erotic videos. You can easily indulge this desire by going to your nearest video store and renting one of the films we recommend.

Take your own test. Watch an erotic tape with another person, or alone, and after twenty minutes ask yourself if you're turned on. Be honest.

We already know the answer to that one.

Chapter 4

Where to Look

The best place to rent erotic films is at your local video store. Some of the bigger chains, like Blockbuster, have a policy of not carrying the hard stuff, and in fact even have edited versions of the steamier R-rated tapes.

But in most communities, there will be a regular mom-and-pop video store that has an adult-oriented section.

You can tell where it is because it's usually blocked off from the rest of the store, often by swinging bat-wing doors like those found on Wild West saloons. Look inside this room and you will find wall racks filled with video boxes featuring naked men and women in various sexual attitudes. That's how you can tell you're in the right place.

Sometimes the stores have special sections that are not blocked off (this requires more guts on the part of the browser) where you stand at a counter and leaf through large books with the video boxes cut apart and laminated on the pages. Sometimes it's just a notebook of loose-leaf pages with titles and brief descriptions. You tell the clerk the number you want and he fetches it for you.

You might find a whole store that rents nothing but these tapes. Look for these emporiums in the sleazier sections of your town, and while they are not the most wholesome and pleasant places to shop, they will most likely have anything you might want.

The point is, if you look around a little you'll find the right place. It's not that difficult. Even if you happen to live in one of those rarefied, sanctimonious communities that has banned all vestiges of modern public sexuality, you can still order videos through the mail or through your home computer. You will find a list of these supply houses and catalogs in chapter fourteen. Buying is a lot more expensive than just renting, though some companies have a buy-and-return policy that comes close to being a rental. If you *are* buying, pay close attention to the reviews in this book so you don't get a film that you spent twenty or thirty dollars on and have to throw away in disgust.

Also men's magazines like *Playboy* and *Penthouse* have vast areas of advertising where X-rated videos are offered for sale. Any sexually oriented material ordered through the mail comes delivered to your door in plain brown wrappers and obscure return addresses, so the mailman is none the wiser.

The erotica industry is huge, bigger than both the mainstream book and movie businesses *combined*. This is at least a $3-billion-a-year business. More than 5,000 erotic videos are produced every year. They wouldn't make that many movies if there were no one watching them. And one last consideration: The movie *Deep Throat*, made in 1972, is still one of the top money grossers in U.S. film history. That's along with *E.T., Star Wars, Jurassic Park, Forrest Gump*, and other mainstream movies. Think about it.

Chapter 5

Tie Me Up?
Tie Me Down?

There are a number of misconceptions that exist about the erotica business, misconceptions that keep people from owning or even viewing this material. We hope all of them will have been dispelled by the time you finish this book.

Some of the most popular beliefs are that there are always scenes of violence against women in these videos, and that the women performers are being forced to participate. The public perception is often one of less-than-healthy acts performed by degraded men and women. This perception is wrong and a far cry from the reality of general-interest, mainstream erotic tapes, those made by big companies and found on the shelves of your local video store. If you want to watch sadomasochistic, misogynistic sex, rent *Basic Instinct*.

The erotic film market caters to a wide variety of tastes, and yes, some of those tastes are sometimes bizarre. But believe me, you'll know those particular tapes when you see their covers, and you can easily avoid them if they are not to your liking.

Erotic films made before the mid-eighties often included a simulated "rape" scene where a woman was forced to have sex with one or more men. This particular scene is seldom found in today's video. When a "rape" is shown there is usually an attempt to incorporate it into the dramatic elements of the story.

But if one is worried about the story content or the performers themselves, the most appropriate consideration is to remember that the people in these films are *actors*. The sex is real, yes, but the situations are fictitious, the context theatrical.

The actors and actresses? The vast majority think of themselves simply as actors and actresses who specialize in erotic films. They have their own professional organizations, maintain strict health standards, and have somewhat standardized pay schedules. A number of special-interest periodicals are solely devoted to the genre, and there are even yearly award ceremonies for best films, actors, and actresses. Most of those involved on either side of the camera are proud and unashamed of their chosen professions. I'm sure there are some who have drug and personal problems, but I would guess that their number is no more, and possibly even less, than those of their counterparts in the traditional Hollywood professions.

There is no reason to feel sorry for these people or look down on them. They are doing exactly what they want to do.

And you're the one who benefits.

Chapter 6

From X to XXXXX

*T*here are a number of different levels of erotic material. They are generally identified by the motion picture rating system that we are all aware of, though there are differences within some of the ratings.

We're not interested in the G, PG, or PG-13 ratings, or even most Rs. Tapes that I consider Hard Rs are films that were released in mainstream theaters and then appeared in the video store in special Director's Cut editions. This almost always means that the sexier material that had to be cut from the general theater release is put back in for the video and/or the European market. I suppose the thinking here is that the American people, simple folk that we are, are able to handle sex in the privacy of our own homes, but not in a public place like a movie theater. Like most policies of this nature, the reasoning is absurd. *Basic Instinct, Indecent Exposure,* and *9½ Weeks* have had Director's Cut editions.

As I said earlier, I think it's unnecessary to bother renting these films just to see a few more brief flashes of nudity. (Sometimes the nude bodies are body doubles, so you're not even seeing the famous star anyway.) If you haven't seen the film at all, then go ahead and rent the director's cut. But don't bother doing so for a pure erotic rush.

The NC-17 designation was invented to exempt films with high sex content from being relegated to the shelves with "pornography." But many theaters, particularly those in suburban shopping malls, are restricted from showing films with this rating, and many newspapers will not carry advertising for this type of film.

The prime example, and first film to be rated in this manner, was *Henry and June*, the fictionalized account of Anaïs Nin's sexual awakening and affair with Henry Miller, set in Paris in the 1930s. I think this is a terrific movie: intelligent, sexy, and funny. Unfortunately, it did not achieve the sort of success it deserved, primarily because of the kiss-of-death NC-17 rating. I recommend the film highly, for the sexual aspects as well as the dramatic content. But how many times can you watch *Henry and June*? Eventually you're going to want to move on.

Showgirls is another film with an NC-17 rating. In this case the rating was actually courted—the thinking being that it would lure in viewers with the promise of hot sex. I'm happy to say that the movie bombed. Not only was it a poorly acted, silly movie, the sex wasn't particularly exciting. It certainly wasn't hot. Intelligent viewers who are interested in sex are now learning that there is a whole section of videos that deliver the real stuff.

Many videos have the designation Not Rated. This means that the filmmakers knew they were not going to make the coveted R rating, so they didn't even try, opting out of the process completely. These are movies I call Soft Xs and you'll find a number of them discussed in the Review Section. Generally this means there will be lots of sexual situations, a generous amount of female nudity (usually above the waist and from the rear), and a small amount of male nudity. An example of this type is the *Red Shoe Diaries* series, the series of films and cable shows that really proved that this could be a big market. The videos offered by the *Playboy* and *Penthouse* companies are harder than an R and yet softer than the Xs.

In some video stores these tapes aren't even shelved back in the Forbidden Zone. They are the moving picture equivalent of the still pictures one finds in men's magazines. There are off-shoots of this type that feature lingerie fashion shows, stripteasing, and other soft sexual themes. There are few naked men, no erections, and no actual penetration. If you feel that you want to put your toe in the water rather than just jumping in, these films are fine.

The sexiest level of erotic videos is the X rating. These are the tapes that are separated in some way from the average browser in the video store. This material shows actual sexual situations, full nudity of both sexes, penetration, ejaculation, and a variety of sex acts ranging from common to kinky. These are the tapes we feel are the most erotically stimulating and those in which the reader will be most interested.

There is no difference in sexual level between an X and an XXX or even an XXXXXX. The difference in the number of Xs exists only in the minds of advertisers and marketing directors and has nothing to do with the MPAA ratings board.

A special category of tapes are those of the Educational type. In the pages of many magazines, from *Playboy* to *The New York Times Book Review*, you'll see advertisements for videos that promise to teach the viewers useful techniques for making love. These tapes are sold for educational—the ads suggest—rather than recreational purposes. The tapes themselves are earnest and tasteful. And they often *do* teach you a thing or two. The types of tapes can range from male and female how-to-masturbate videos to sensual massage techniques to clinical analyses of sexual dysfunctions. Most of them, though, concentrate on showing techniques that will simply enhance the pleasures of making love.

If you feel like this is a good way to break into the world of adult films, by all means go ahead and rent some of these tapes. Most video stores have them, but we don't feel you actually need to buy the series. We feel that while the ads overstate their case, the tapes themselves are pleasant to watch. Personally, we like our sex a little less sanitized.

Chapter 7

Why We Like to Watch

There is no question that almost all heterosexual men like to look at pictures of beautiful naked women. An enormous industry supports this conclusion. And the one thing men like better than looking at still pictures of naked women is looking at moving pictures of naked women. Another enormous industry supports this fact. But do women also enjoy seeing pictures and films of naked people?

I think the answer is yes, but they enjoy them in a different way than men do.

Most studies show a rather simple fact: In sexual situations, men are very direct and primarily visual. They base their responses on what they actually see: Is their partner good-looking, does she have attractive breasts, legs, etc., while women's reactions are based on a broader spectrum, incorporating a much larger range of senses and emotions in their sexual responses. This means, to approach it on a rather formulaic level, that men are turned on by looking at unfiltered physical sex, and women are turned on by experiencing the more emotional side of sex: candles, courtship, and romance.

This would lead us to believe that adult films are geared primarily to men's enjoyment—and basically, this seems to be true. The preponderance of tapes are aimed at men who are watching the tape alone: We call these single-guy tapes. But more and more tapes are being produced that are aimed at couples, and we find that many women not only like them, but find them very exciting. Full-spectrum sexuality includes watching and listening, as well as the involvement of all the other senses. In reality, our sexual responses are varied and complex, a mixture of many sensual elements. Add watching people making love to the mix, and you'll set a powerful reaction from both sexes.

Here is the bottom line: If you watch the best of these movies you're going to be turned on. And everybody likes to be turned on.

The world of erotic films is not a closely held secret. Millions of people enjoy these films. But the commonly accepted stereotype of the average viewer, and the commonly held stereotype of the average tape, have kept large segments of the population away from this unique pleasure.

It's time for those stereotypes to be buried.

The video sales and rental business was born when videocassettes and players became commonly available. No longer were we condemned to watching dull weekend-night television—we could go to the store and choose a movie. It was an entertainment form perfect for couples with children. It was cheap, easily available, you weren't required to dress up, and you didn't have to hire a baby-sitter.

Video stores, independents and chains, sprung up like crabgrass in a spring lawn. Every strip mall, every downtown, every suburb had at least one video store. After the industry sorted out the Beta vs. VHS controversy and dropped the membership fees, renting a tape was as easy as putting on your shoes and driving to the liquor store.

Home erotica, long the province of super-eight films shown in smoke-filled garages and basements, moved to the middle-class bedroom. Curious men and women could rent this stuff from the local video store and bring it home and watch it in private.

My local video store has around four hundred sex tapes for rent, and several tallies over several weeks show that on Friday and Saturday nights, approximately three hundred of these tapes are off the shelves *each night*. And even during the week the number is a lot higher than you might imagine, considering people have to get up and go to work the next morning. These are rentals by men and women who live in a family-oriented community in a typical suburb. No one drives out from the city to our placid neighborhood to rent X-rated tapes. Suffice it to say, we are hardly a hotbed of perverts.

Most of the customers I see renting tapes are men. But more and more, I am beginning to see women in the adult section, sometimes with men, sometimes alone. A study of one thousand video stores done in 1986 showed that slightly more than 50 percent of erotic videos were rented either by women alone or by men and women as couples. A recent issue of *Men's Health* magazine put the statistic at one-third. Whichever study is correct, this is good news, because it shows that the erotic film industry has been correct in moving away from single-guy films, and toward their ultimate goal, the couple's market. Though you will still find that a majority of the films available are geared to a solo male audience, there are many offerings for couples.

Chapter 8

The Couple's Tape: Tell Me a Story

*F*or several years many producers in the erotic film industry have declared the couple's video as one of their chief priorities. The rock-solid market of lonely guys watching X-rated tapes and pursuing solitary pleasures was considered safe, but with limited growth potential. This consistently lucrative business was not enough—the producers decided to cultivate a more discerning and demanding segment of the population : women.

Women weren't going to go for the in-your-face, industrial-strength sex that most of the guys readily accepted. Women liked a story line, good-looking performers, decent production values, and more buildup to the ultimate scenes.

To us, the most important element in a couple's tape *is* the story. A story puts the sexual material in a framework that we can easily understand and relate to. Story supplies a buildup of interest and atmosphere. We are led into the relationships between the characters and thereby understand the sexual situations. Many erotic videotapes have no story at all, and many that do have only the poorest excuse for anything that might be considered a plot. For many people, mostly single-guy viewers, this lack doesn't really matter. They feel that a story only gets in the way of the real point of an erotic film, namely, the sex. But we feel that a plot, even the most inane, makes the viewing experience much more powerful and appealing.

In the succinct and powerful words of my wife and fellow reviewer when faced with yet another wall to waller (see glossary), "Oh no, not another one with just dicks and pussies."

The real power of the modern erotic video is to produce in the viewer an electric, almost instantaneous jolt of desire, and I, for one, am not always willing to follow a complicated story line when my attentions are focused elsewhere. This, I think we've mentioned, is probably a predominantly male point of view.

But most of the tapes we consider to be couples-oriented efforts have some sort of story line. This varies from the cliches of a young woman being initiated into the glories of a sexual life, to mate swapping, to the wackiest themes you could ever imagine.

Often the stories are so ridiculous, the dialogue and setting so silly that the result is comedy, sometimes intentional, sometimes not. Nothing wrong with that. Laughter and sex go together nicely, and in fact, laughter can often smooth over some couples' initial embarrassment at viewing these tapes. If it's too ridiculous, just turn it off and next time rent something by someone else. Remember our mantra: There's always another tape to rent.

But in the best of these tapes, the story is a comfortable fit with all the other elements and the viewer is rewarded with an entertaining and stimulating experience, with the emphasis on the stimulating. Characters, story, setting, and atmosphere all connect to draw the viewers into the fictional sexual world, which in turn encourages and draws them into their own romantic encounter.

Chapter 9

Renting the Tape: Short Cuts and Tips

Many first-time renters have difficulty with the idea of being seen in public renting an erotic video. This makes sense: Many people have been brought up to view any public interest in sex as shameful. If you're the sort of person, however, who can buy an erotic magazine or tape without qualms, great, you may skip the rest of this chapter.

I have to admit, I've been renting these movies for several years now and I still check the store to see who's there before I slip into The Forbidden Zone. And I check it again on the way out. I can't help it, but I don't let it stop me, and if I do see someone, say the grade-school principal, I hang around until he's rented his tape and is on his way. Then I get mine. Maybe this just adds to the excitement.

There are several ways to deal with this.

- You can go to a different part of town so you don't run into any neighbors or friends.
- You can buy mail order, though you can't rent that way.
- You can go to the store during off-hours. If you show up at 7:30 on a Friday or Saturday night to rent adult material,

the store is going to be crowded—so go on your lunch hour if possible, or as soon as you get home from work.
- You can also make your mate or partner go rent the film. Renting seems to be easier for men than most women, although some women say they get a sense of empowerment from it. If you're female, just tell yourself as you approach the counterperson, "I Am Woman, Hear Me Roar . . ."
- Or, you can just say, I don't give a damn what anyone thinks, and go to the store and rent what you want. That's the best way. Man or woman. (It helps if you've read up in the review section so you know some names before you show up. Otherwise you're going to spend some time looking at every box until you find something that seems worth renting.)

Then there's the counterperson. In the mom-and-pop type of video store, you're quite likely to get Mom or Pop waiting on you. I could drag this out, but the person waiting on you really doesn't care what you're renting. If they own the place, they're glad to get the money. X-rated tapes usually have a slightly higher rental fee anyway. If they just work there, they're thinking about what they're going to do when they get home. These people, owners or employees, are not passing judgment. They honestly don't care.

Let's assume that you've decided to go ahead and rent a tape. You've gone in the store and made your way back to The Forbidden Zone. Before you left home, you studied the review section of this book and memorized a list of ten films. You look around. You're surrounded by hundreds of boxes with naked men and women on them. They all seem to have goofy names. You're nervous. Suddenly, you realize that you've forgotten all the titles you memorized.

Hopefully, you've read this entire book and know how to pick a tape without having a specific title to guide you. And next

time, write the names on a small piece of paper, or even bring
this book with you.

Here are some shortcuts and tips for picking a tape. We recommend you read the rest of this book, including the reviews,
for the big picture, but when in doubt, remember the following
pointers.

- First of all, read the box. Perhaps the foremost clue in
  your search for a couple's film is to look for tapes originally
  shot on film. Everyone knows that 35-mm film—with the
  required attendant equipment and personnel—is more expensive than videotape. And the added expense shows:
  Film almost always looks better. Not *every* erotic video
  shot on film is good, but the quality of those that are is
  almost always higher than those shot on tape. Not the
  physical quality—the medium of videotape is physically
  equal to film—but the intellectual and production quality.
  If it was shot on film, they'll say so on the box because
  it's a selling point for the in-the-know consumer.

After pondering the reasons for some time, we've decided
that tape has a brightness about it, a clarity, that just doesn't
look as good as film. You see too much with tape, and in
erotica where you see everything, too much is not necessarily a good thing.

An element of mystery is extremely important in pro-
jecting sexuality. This is as true on a tape as it is in person.
Some things should not be so clear that they distract.

There's also the element of sound. Of all the production
values in videotapes, it seems that sound suffers most. In
some tapes, the sound is so bad the dialogue is virtually
incomprehensible. Good sound requires expensive boom
mikes at the very least. But in most tape productions, the
sound guy has only a hand-held mike to catch everything.

Often, what you get is a loudness that catches every creak and footstep, every piece of ambient sound, all of which distracts rather than enhances.

I believe that there's also a psychological aspect that comes with using film that also affects the product. A small percentage of the professional performers do most of the movies. They don't really make all that much money, so they have to take the work when it is available. They usually get paid the same whether they're on film or tape, so it doesn't help them to hold out for the more expensive medium. But I feel they try harder, put more into their acting when they have decent costumes, good sets, a creative director, and a production company that's willing to part with some extra money to get a first-class effect. I believe it shows in the end.

Now comes the inevitable caveat: Not all film-shot videos are great. And not all tape efforts are bad. In general, as noted elsewhere, if in doubt, rent the tape that was originally shot on film.

- Check for any other boasts about the quality of equipment, i.e., "Shot with Betacam SP." Remember this rule: The more money that goes into making the tape, the better the quality, and they almost always brag about it on the cover.
- No heavily tattooed women. Small tattoos can be cool, and even a smiley face can be good for a laugh. Like it or not, ever since Cher decided to tattoo herself, women everywhere have followed her example. A good rule to follow: The smaller the tattoo, the better, and large tattoos indicate lousy films—don't bother to rent. I know this sounds like a personal, completely idiosyncratic rule, and maybe it is, but we've seen a lot of these films, and it's just a turnoff, at least to us, to see a woman covered in tattoos.
- No ugly guys. No ugly women. There are so many fine-

looking actors and actresses in this business there's really no point in looking at anything less than first-class bodies and faces. Unless you're into that sort of thing.

- No black socks and no sunglasses. For some reason, in the old days, this outfit, or lack of outfit, used to be de rigueur in what were called Blue movies (so named as the film often had a blue tint). You can still rent examples of these early porn films, and watching them has a certain academic interest, but in general they have little to recommend them. The viewing quality is usually extremely poor, there is no story or even much connecting material, and the performers are usually not very good looking. Sometimes in today's erotic films you'll see the guys wearing their sunglasses, or even keeping on their socks. I can almost stand the sunglasses—maybe the movie lights are bright—but I won't watch a film where the guys have on their socks. How can you tell what footgear is going to be worn in a film before you rent it? Again, look at the little pictures on the box. They won't show you everything inside, but they give a pretty good indication. If you don't like the pictures, don't rent the film. There are many, many more to choose from.

- Sometimes, they'll try to trick you by putting pictures on the box that don't have anything to do with the film. That's one of the reasons there's a review section in this book. But the more scrupulous producers will often have a notation on the box saying "Pictures on box depict performers on tape." Look for it. If it isn't there, it doesn't necessarily mean you're about to be cheated, but it's nice to see it when you're judging possible quality strictly from the box.

- Also, there should be a short blurb describing the plot as well. Sometimes it's just a promise of how hot that particular tape is going to get you, but other times it offers a good description of the pleasures within. At the very least, you can check out the cast list. As you watch more videos, you'll find that some performers especially turn you on. If the video is aimed primarily at the couple's market, it usually says so prominently. As with any movie, reviews and accolades quoted on the cover are a good sign.

That's the short form: read the box. To really learn how to tell the good from the bad, read the rest of this book.

Chapter 10

Professionals and Amateurs: Who's on Top?

Y ou'll find that there are two distinct types of productions: the professionally produced tape, and the amateur-produced tape.

Beth and I both feel that it's best to start with the professional production companies. VCA, Vivid, and many others all offer well made, high-quality productions. But, beware: many of their efforts are too nasty, in their parlance, to be considered couple's material. (When erotic film production people, directors, actresses, and actors use the word *nasty* they usually mean tapes that are short on story and atmosphere and long on the hardcore elements: anal sex, gang bangs, double penetrations, odd-looking participants, etc.)

The point is that even when showcasing these nasty elements, the big companies can turn out a tape that has excellent production values. By applying the various tips in this book and using the reviews, couples can avoid material that they might find too extreme.

On the other hand, the advent of high-quality tape recording equipment has made it possible for anyone with a minimal amount of money to put together an erotic tape and offer it for sale. The market is so huge, and in many respects undemanding, or rather omnidemanding, that even extremely amateurish tapes can make it onto the shelves of your local video store. These tapes are part of the rapidly expanding amateur market.

As we said, we feel you should start with the pros. Professionally produced tapes look professional, and amateur tapes look, well, much of the time, amateur, particularly in the areas of performer attractiveness and plot coherence. The high quality of the equipment, performers, and plot in professional erotica stands head and shoulders above the average person and his camcorder. And if you're looking for story, amateur tapes usually offer no story at all.

When you start off watching erotic tapes, especially if you're trying to win over a reluctant partner, you want good-looking people making love in attractive ways with all the better production values evident. Later on, when you know what you're doing and you've refined your tastes, you can dip into the more specialized worlds, but until then, start with the mainstream.

Here's the way producing a mainstream erotic video usually works. The producers raise the money to make a film. They go to a tried-and-true director and give him the money, usually around $15,000, sometimes as little as $10,000. He makes the movie, pays for the equipment, the locations, and the performers. His pay is whatever's left over.

This method does not encourage lavish productions.

It is also true that the larger portion of the audience, single guys sitting alone at home, doesn't care about frills. They want people screwing in many different ways, and that's about it. If I'm offending anyone's sensibilities out there, sorry, but that's the way it is.

The director John T. Bone once said something to the effect that it was difficult for him to expend the time, energy, and money on a classy 35-mm film project when he could make twice as much money on an all-anal cheapie made with a Hi-8 camera. Perhaps with the growth of the couple's market we will see that particular trend change.

Most professional hard-core tapes and films are now made in two separate versions, just as many mainstream movies are shot in two different versions, with the sexier edition for European markets. Erotic tapes as well are now shot in hard and soft. The soft versions are made for cable TV and the hotel business. The explicit sex is edited out as well as some of the more graphic dialogue, or, in many cases, the scenes are shot twice, once with everything showing, and then with the more graphic elements simply not shown. There are no erect penises allowed, in fact very few penises at all, and there is no semen. While they do have full-frontal female nudity, there are no close-ups of genitalia.

One area where film is never used is in amateur productions. Because of our bias toward film vs. tape, we didn't think we would like watching amateur videos as much as we do, but when they are done well, they are a terrific turn-on. Do you have a fantasy about your next-door neighbor or co-worker? Rent an amateur tape; odds are there's a man or woman who looks exactly like them, or someone you know. I could swear I saw my local librarian in one.

Amateur videos are like your very own more mundane fantasies come to life. Forget the gauzy, slo-mo fantasies of you in bed with a bunch of terrific-looking sex partners. These are real people, having real, sometimes awkward sex, with often real orgasms. It's nice to see genuine shyness between lovers. Some tapes are done as fantasies, some are filmed orgies, others are more personal. Most of the tapes do not have a musical soundtrack, and many scenes are all-the-more erotic with genuine sounds of lovemaking. When there is music, it's often either cheesy synth music or popular rock songs pirated right off the radio. Bruce Springsteen, call your lawyer.

One of the most appealing aspects of the amateur genre, at least to me, is the constant effort on the part of each partner to try and please the other. Professionals can be hot, or they can be cold, but seldom are they accommodating. While the amateurs are also trying to make a tape that will appeal to an audience, they forget easily and slip back into the habits of love and marriage. Professionals never forget. They always play to the camera. Amateurs try to please us, but mostly they please themselves. When they say they love each other, it isn't scripted. They mean it. You can overlook a lot of flabby bellies when people are sincere and caring.

After watching amateur for a while I realized that another reason I stayed with it was that you never really knew what the people were going to do next. With the pros, you usually know exactly what's going to happen: Boy meets girl, blow job, cunnilingus, missionary, rear entry, sometimes anal, pull out, cum shot. Certainly not a bad repertoire, but it can become a little predictable.

With the amateurs, you never know what they're going to say or do. You never know what the next one is going to look like. Sometimes the uncertainty leads to something good, sometimes to something you'd rather not see. Not knowing makes it interesting.

Take a chance and try out some amateur. These no-budget efforts can sometimes be hotter than professional erotica. But, like I said, only when they are done skillfully. When they are done poorly, they are a horrific turnoff. Bad camera work, unattractive partners, or outlandish fetishes can ruin an evening. However, amateur tapes tell you straight out what you're getting: interracial, lesbian, bi, old, fat, skinny, hairy, beautiful, or depraved. You won't get tricked here. There were a lot of people on these tapes I wished had kept their sex lives to themselves, but then, there's also quite a few I'm glad invited me along.

Amateur tape distribution is a rapidly expanding area of the business. Most of the tapes labeled amateur in the rental stores are really pro-am efforts. Pro-am videos combine professional actors and actresses with amateurs hoping to break into the business. It's a nice turn-on to see your favorites performing with unknowns. Real amateur tapes are more expensive to distribute and cost the retailers more to shelve. So generally they skip them. You can purchase them through mail-order outlets, several of which we recommend in a later chapter. Most of the amateur tape companies will sell you a compilation tape that gives you some short scenes from videos in their catalogue. This is extremely helpful because there are a lot of performers and situations that you're not going to want to look at.

Chapter 11

Actors, Actresses, and Directors

A good way to choose a tape is to pick one that stars your favorite performers. But it should always be understood that these stars might appear one day in the *Gone with the Wind* of erotica and the next day star in a raunchy all-anal buttfest that will have you opening the windows and airing out the house after you watch it. It's the nature of their business. They don't get to sit around and read scripts and take the high road; most of them will act in whatever opportunity comes their way. Someday this may change, but at this stage of the business they take the work when it's offered.

So while you usually know some basic facts—that you like a certain person's looks, or that Janine does only women—you can never be sure of quality from a certain performer's presence in a tape. If you like a performer, it's a good reason to pick up the box and see what the tape is all about. I will watch any movie with Ashlyn Gere, and Beth can find no wrong in Rocco Sefreddi's work. And when they appear together, there's no stopping us from putting the kids to bed early.

The Women

After years of being underlings in this male-dominated business, women are beginning to take the first steps toward holding the reins as both performers and directors. Some of them, the Contract Girls, women under special exclusive contracts with specific studios, are becoming so powerful that even directors must do what they ask. By signing these contracts they receive good salaries and often the right to stipulate with whom they will perform, and in which scripts. But the Contract Girls are a very small minority in a very large business. Most women work for low wages and have absolutely no say in who they work with or the quality of the scripts, or even if there is a script.

A large percentage of the women are primarily dancers who work a nationwide circuit of adult clubs. It is possible for them to vastly increase their salaries and tips in these clubs after they've been on a few video box covers. Some of them can make as much as ten thousand dollars a week in the clubs, and thousands of dollars per week is not unusual for a woman who has done erotic videos. The pay scale on a shoot is also extremely variable, with top-rank female stars able to earn thousands of dollars a day, though this is far from the norm.

There seem to be, at least to us as viewers, around twenty or so actresses who are doing most of the work. We've made a short list of some of the women we have liked in the past. Included are some whom we don't necessarily recommend, but are interesting for other reasons. Here, as with the tapes themselves, personal preferences are sure to vary.

We find we end up liking certain performers for quirky reasons as well as the obvious ones. Most of the women are at least attractive, and many are stunningly beautiful. I value enthusiasm above almost all other attributes. I am quickly bored, and turned off, by women who seem to be putting in the time for the video credits to boost their dancing career rather than taking any enjoyment from their participation. Once is enough with these actresses and I don't usually rent movies they're in unless there are other attractions.

But many performers dive into their roles with enthusiastic abandon, and this often seems to light a fire under not only their partners, but the rest of the cast as well. A beautiful woman who seems genuinely turned on can turn even a completely plotless effort into an exciting evening.

Here are some that we like.

Julia Ann - Julia is a fabulously beautiful, blond erotica star who appears in a number of our favorite tapes. She's a former Penthouse Pet who is a regular on the national dance circuit where she performs with another favorite of ours, Janine, in a duo known as Blondage. She first appeared in one of our most-recommended tapes, Andrew Blake's *Hidden Obsessions*, where she won an X-rated Critics Organization award for Best Girl-Girl Scene of 1993. She performed her first scene with a man in another highly recommended Blake film, *Les Femmes Erotique.*

Juli Ashton - Juli has had a couple of name changes since she started in the business, but she appears under the name Ashton in some of the tapes we've liked. She has a sort of smirk that I find sexy, besides having a great body with (at least for now) natural breasts. She's in Michael Ninn's *Latex*, and if you want a rougher Juli Ashton experience, look for her in various combinations in Greg Dark's *DMJ5: The Inferno.* (Note: the title of this film stands for Devil in Miss Jones. Now you're in the cognoscenti and can toss around terms like DMJ5.)

Asia Carrera - Part Asian, Asia has a natural body and a certain grace that makes most of her performances compelling. Her great qualities are evident in the actual sexual parts of her performance, rather than in the parts where she's "acting." Then she's often perfectly ordinary, just another of the foul-mouthed girls. The thing is, you never can be really sure about her tapes. Her individual quality rises and falls with the quality of the script. Generally, though, we like her. She's married to erotic tape director Bud Lee. Two of the movies we've liked her in and which are reviewed herein are *Sex* and *R & R*.

Celeste - Now retired (for the second time), Celeste starred in *Borderline*, as well as several other of our picks in the review section. She's a brunette, for a nice change, and she has a natural body that silicone could never improve upon. She's in four of our reviewed tapes, *Borderline, Hidden Obsessions, Immortal Desire,* and *Elements of Desire*. She's a beautiful woman who can act, given the opportunity. Let's hope she isn't permanently retired.

Jeanna Fine - We can never decide if we really like Jeanna Fine, but as she keeps cropping up in our most-liked reviews, I guess we do. She's come and gone a number of times in the business, and we prefer her in her latest reincarnation where she can be recognized by her new short hairdo. She certainly seems willing to do just about anything sexwise, and she can also act. She won Performer of the Year from the X-Rated Critics Organization and several awards for her appearance in *Brandy and Alexander*, a movie often cited as one of the best ever, but which has also never appeared in our video store. We're still looking for it. If, like us, you can't find *Brandy and Alexander*, we recommend her in *House of Dreams, Sex Lives of Clowns, DMJ5: The Inferno, Latex, Blue Movie,* and others.

Ashlyn Gere - One of the great adult film stars and one of the few to cross over into mainstream work, Ashlyn has made appearances on *The X-Files* and *Space: Above and Beyond* series on the Fox television network. She gives an outstanding performance, both sexual and as an actress, in the sequel to *The Masseuse*, and starred in one of the first erotic videos we ever saw, and highly recommend, *Chameleons*.

Sarah Jane Hamilton - Sarah Jane is a British import who's recently had her breasts enlarged. Attractive and bouncy rather than beautiful, she's primarily known for her ability to "squirt." Squirting, or female ejaculation, is an interesting phenomenon exhibited by a few of the erotica stars. Controversy surrounds this spectacle with some saying it's always faked and others swearing it's legitimate. Watch Sarah Jane do her thing in our recommended *Immortal Desire* or *Sex Lives of Clowns* and decide for yourselves.

Nina Hartley - One of the champions of responsible erotica, Nina is a former nurse and counts First Amendment rights and health awareness as two of her particular concerns. She's appeared in more than 450 erotic videos and has begun directing as well as acting in a series of how-to videos, one of which we recommend, *Nina Hartley's Guide to Better Fellatio*. Most of her other tapes are a little hard for our tastes, but she deserves a lot of credit for trying to upgrade the adult erotica environment. Watching a Nina Hartley tape every once in a while is more an act of supportive politics than a sensual experience, but sometimes sacrifices have to be made by all of us.

Janine - As of this writing, the lovely Janine, a former Penthouse Pet, has sex (on camera) only with women. We find her bosom too large, but that's the case with most of these ladies, and a purely personal preference. She's always extremely elegant, winner of the 1993 Best Girl-Girl Scene in Andrew Blake's *Hidden Obsessions*, and one-half the dance team, Blondage. She's as beautiful as any woman could be, and if hard-core erotica fans are miffed because she only performs sexually with women, too bad, be thankful for what you've got. We recommend her in *Hidden Obsessions* and *Blonde Justice*.

Traci Lords - Traci is famous primarily because she made more than a hundred movies between 1983 and 1986 while she was underage. When it became known, the movies she was in were taken off the shelves and in some cases re-edited so she did not appear. Several movies made after she became of age are available. She is another of the few adult stars who has begun to make appearances outside the business, appearing on television in *Married . . . With Children*, *Roseanne*, *Melrose Place*, and a num-

ber of Hollywood B movies. While we don't particularly recommend her or her videos because she's one of the women who
are too hard-core for our tastes, she's interesting because of her
underage performances and how those appearances changed the
business.

Tyffany Million - Tyffany (her name is spelled a number of
different ways in different films) is one of erotica's hardest-
working professionals. Blond, with an extremely fit body, she's
an award winner in Michael Ninn's *Sex*, one of our highly recommended films. She is also one of the few women stars who
has started her own company (Immaculate Video Conceptions)
and moved behind the camera. While Tyffany is still an active
performer, she has produced her own line of tapes that are supposedly aimed at women without losing the hard-core edge that
men seem to prefer. We viewed a number of these tapes, and
as yet have found little to distinguish them from the general
run-of-the-mill single-guy erotica. As a performer, though, Tyffany is first rate and has appeared in many tapes since her start
in 1990. We liked her in *Face Dance I and II*, *American Garter*,
Borderline, *Climax 2000*, *Exstasy*, and others.

Lacey Rose - While not the most beautiful woman in the business, Lacey has a full-tilt style that is riveting. She embodies
the word enthusiasm. She's a tall brunette with man-made
breasts, but even the silicone can't dampen my enthusiasm for
her over-the-top performances. I've never seen her in any tape,
even ones we don't recommend, where she doesn't appear to be
totally out of her mind with lust. We recommend her in *The Reel
World*.

Amateur Women - As a whole, the women are pretty good-
looking, usually tending toward one's nice-looking next-door
neighbor rather than drop-dead beautiful. It must be said,
though, that many of the women are, to be honest, not very
attractive or have bodies that are, to put it kindly, flawed. Different companies showcase different women and a quick look at

their compilation tape will usually tell you if their idea of beautiful or sexy corresponds with yours. Be careful.

The Men

The pay for male performers is much lower than for female. For one thing, there is no male dance circuit for the men to build a large viewer base. Most men are paid from one to three hundred dollars a day. For this they may be expected to perform in as many as three or more scenes.

Because of the inequity of the pay, many of the top actors branch out into directorial roles. Once seen as the next step for men who were no longer able to perform on camera, directing has now been recognized for the lucrative opportunities it offers. Most of the actors feel that they are already doing the really hard part, so why not direct and be well compensated for it?

There are several questions people always ask about the men in these films. One of them is, Do they have really big penises? The answer is no, not all of them, even though most of them look really big.

It's often a matter of camera angles. The definitive answer was given by Ernest Hemingway to a concerned F. Scott Fitzgerald. Hemingway said many men feel they are small compared to others because they only see themselves while looking down while at the urinal. This foreshortens the view.

But the answer is also yes, some of the guys are *really* big. Check out Rocco Sefreddi, Sean Michaels, Tom Byron, and Peter North for four that are quite large. And also note that erotic productions don't usually showcase guys with small penises.

An example of too much of a good thing has to be Long Dong Silver. He's also an example of how easily most of us can be hoaxed. Even Supreme Court justices.

Both Beth and I have always wondered about Long Dong, at least after we heard about him as part of the Clarence Thomas/ Anita Hill hearings. Then, while researching my mystery book,

I rented the erotica tape *Beauty and the Beast*. There, in all his lengthy glory, was Long Dong. We were amazed. A youngish African-American, we saw him dance around a stage swinging a semi-erect penis that was literally two feet long. In a later scene he has sex with the legendary Seka, who manages to stuff in more than a foot of his organ. Pretty amazing.

While doing the research for this book, I learned, sadly, it was all a fake. Rubber, it turns out. In fact most of the oddities one sees are fraudulent.

Except for a few, most guys are pretty much the same size.

Here are some men we like, and some we don't.

Buck Adams - Buck is a longtime star, now directing more than acting. He's the brother of female star Amber Lynn and a Kirk Douglas lookalike who is great in tough-guy roles. He can act and he is a dependable woodsman, two features that put him above many of the other male erotica stars. We recommend his performance, even though he plays an unsympathetic character, in *R & R*.

John Wayne Bobbitt - Is there any man or woman alive who does not know John's story? Among male performers, he remains alone in what must be the business's smallest niche market. Known as a poor performer (serious erection problems), he nonetheless won a number of awards at the 1995 Adult Video News Awards: Best-Renting Tape of the Year, Best-Selling Tape of the Year, Best Overall Marketing Campaign. Thus proving that the public's thirst for the bizarre knows no bounds.

The buzz has it that on John's first tape, *Uncut*, he struggled for days with his erection problems. Finally, the producers took a hand and had John injected with prostaglandin, a fatty acid that produces an erection. Over the next several days, he managed five cum shots, each produced with the help of the prostaglandin. We recommend that you never rent a John Bobbitt tape, both for his inadequacies as a performer and his well-documented past.

T. T. Boy - One of the real superwoodsmen in the business, known for his ability to get it up, and get it off, all on command. While his acting repertoire is severely limited, to put it kindly, he is able to summon the proper attitude time after time and show no signs of flagging. T. T. has made more than eight hundred films since entering the business in 1990. He's good-looking, but no Cary Grant by any means. We find him too rough with his partners for our taste, but it's hard to rent a tape where he won't pop up at some point. You can see him do his thing in *The Secret Garden, Bonnie and Clyde, DMJ5: The Inferno, Erotika,* and *Sinderella.*

Mark Davis - Mark is an attractive guy who doesn't show up in as many films as his erotica brethren. Tall and well endowed, he has a kind of British charm that translates into hot sexuality when he's involved in higher-class efforts. Women like watching him perform. Catch him in *The Dinner Party.*

Jon Dough - One of the men who can really act, Jon stars in two of our top picks, *Sex* and *Latex,* though he's in many more of our recommended tapes. He has made more than six hundred tapes since 1987 so he's well represented. He stars in more demanding roles than any other actor, often playing characters with physical or mental disabilities, and seems to enjoy stretching the limits of being an erotic actor. The only thing we don't like about Jon Dough is his propensity to spank his partners on occasion, though none of the ladies ever seems to complain. We are, though: Stop it, Jon, it isn't really all that sexy.

Nick East - Every time I see Nick East in a tape I think of the young Michael Landon as Little Joe. East is in a lot of the sleazier stuff, but then all the guys are in a lot of the sleazier stuff. Most of the women as well. We liked East in *American Garter,* and *Justine: Nothing To Hide,* where he shows he can act as well as perform sexually.

Mike Horner - Horner, at least to Beth and me, always seems out of place in these movies. He looks like a regular guy who plays regular older-guy types of roles, and in *Justine: Nothing To Hide*, he proves he can act as well as any Hollywood performer. Proof that he's just as adept as any of the other guys is the fact that he was voted into the X-rated Critics Organization Hall of Fame in 1992 and received a Free Speech Coalition Lifetime Achievement Award in 1995. His directorial effort *Tangled*, in our estimation, is an offbeat classic. We await more of his behind-the-camera work.

Ron Jeremy - Ron has appeared in more than one thousand films, ranging from the earliest Golden Age classics to the latest 251-man gang bang. Aside from being in so many tapes, he is known for his now-rotund figure, his nickname "the Hedgehog," and his ability to auto-fellate. We don't recommend you run out and rent a Ron Jeremy tape, but the man's a legend in the industry and if you want to catch his solo sex act, check it out in a brief scene in *The Devil In Miss Jones II*. It's worth the rental.

John Leslie - Leslie appears as an actor in older, Golden Age films, where he was considered the consummate performer. We agree. He's leading-man handsome and can really act. Nowadays he's a director who sometimes takes a non-sex role in his artier efforts, such as *The Dog Walker*, where he plays Dennis Hopper to perfection. He also does the voice-over in his not-recommended *Voyeur* series, although the audience never sees him. Read more about him in the Directors section.

Sean Michaels - Sean is the premier African-American adult performer. Pick up any black or interracial tape and he is usually in it. He can act, he is good-looking, he has a great body, and he's hung like a stallion. See him as an intelligent performer and great sex partner in *R & R* and in *The Dinner Party*. He also sells his own line of designer briefs.

Johnathan Morgan - Morgan is a Malcolm McDowell look-alike who does his best work in offbeat McDowell-type roles. We think he's the best actor in the business, and he's a perfectly fine sexual performer as well. We thought he was very funny in *American Garter* and hysterical in *Sex Lives of Clowns*. His acting in *Clockwork Orgy* makes everyone else look like amateurs.

Peter North - North is legendary for his ability to produce a veritable fountain with his money shot. He is a stalwart regular who has appeared in more than a thousand tapes and can be relied upon for a creditable performance. He's short, with a hard body and pixieish good looks, though Beth thinks that his legs are too short for his torso. Sheesh, everybody's a critic. North can be seen in three Andrew Blake tapes, *Desire*, *Hidden Obsessions*, and *Les Femmes Erotiques*.

Steven St. Croix - Originally trained as a stone mason, St. Croix turned to stripping, then acting in erotic films. A workmanlike actor who always gets the job done, he appears in more and more tapes every year. His appearance is unusual in that he isn't terribly handsome but his body and equipment are both first-rate. He's not afraid to take chances with his acting. We liked him in *The Dog Walker*, *Blue Movie*, *Borderline*, and *Gangland Bangers*.

Rocco Sefreddi - One of the all-time greats, this Italian star performs in videos all over the world. He is very good-looking and can act, after a fashion. He has his own line of videos now, ones that appear too raw for our tastes. He's a perennial in Stagliano's *Buttman* series, and is likely to turn up just about anywhere in adult video. The first time he pulled out his equipment, Beth sat back and laughed. And not because he's small.

Rocco's roles stretch from beefcake muscleman to studious intellectual with wire-rim glasses. He's in so many tapes we recommend that it would be ridiculous to list them all. For an fictional but fascinating look at the life of a male erotica star, see him in *Facedance*. For a real star turn, watch *Jungle Heat*, where

his Tarzan wardrobe stretches from loincloth to tuxedo to nothing. He looks great in all three.

Jeff Stryker - Jeff is one of the few males who appear in both
gay and hetero tapes and is known, aside from his tape work,
for his line of rubber goods, sexual aids, playing cards, posters,
and magazines. His dildo, the Jeff Stryker Realistic, is the num-
ber-one-selling dildo on the market today. Jeff commands huge
salaries in his gay films, thousands of dollars higher than what
most performers in hetero films make.

Amateur Men - Most of these guys are not very good-looking.
I saw one tape where the male lead looked, swear to God, just
like Mr. Rogers. I watched this whole tape to make sure that he
wasn't going to refer to his partner as his neighbor. I kept waiting
for the mailman, Mr. McFeeley—and isn't that a great porno
name—to bang on the door and tell him he had a package of
marital aids, speedy delivery. I have to admit, though, the guy
was a pretty cool customer. He had a whole arsenal of sex talk
that was a lot better than anything I've ever come up with. I
especially liked how he would say, as he lay on his back with
his friend straddled on top, "Ride it on home, Honey, ride it on
home."

Orgasms

No discussion of the men and women who appear in erotic videos would be complete without including a few words on orgasm. The crowning moment for both the male and the female
performers, orgasm is not taken for granted on a shoot. Well,
let's modify that: No one takes the *men's* orgasms for granted, so
we'll deal with them first.

While it may be easy for most guys to reach the pinnacle in
the privacy of their own homes, it's not easy on the set of an
adult production. Consider all the people standing around: di-

rector, cameraman, soundman, and other actors and actresses. There are often hangers-on. Then there are the fluff girls, the suitcase pimps, and the constant threat of wood breakdown (see glossary).

The sets are often dirty and uncomfortable. Witness all the sex scenes shot on stairways and in bathrooms. The performers are being given instructions while performing: lift her leg, turn her over, pull back her hair. They are told to hurry up or slow down. Does this sound like the ideal situation for producing an orgasm?

No. It's a difficult situation in which to maintain an erection. That's why the best of the male performers appear in so many productions; they are reliable woodsmen who can be depended on for a well-maintained erection and reasonably timed orgasm.

A woman's orgasm can be faked, but can a man's? It's often said that the cum shot, or money shot, is faked. What seems like a small Niagara of semen is said to be Ivory Liquid Soap or that production favorite, Dream Creme Rinse. But in watching lots of these movies, I've yet to see a cum scene that I thought was indisputably faked (besides the megasplash scene in *Latex*, see review), and the vast majority of them were indisputably *not* faked. So let's hear a round of applause for our male adult film performers, who work under difficult conditions and still see the job through to the end.

Because of the difficulty of the job, the same six or seven men seem to perform in 80 or 90 percent of the movies. And some of them have been around for at least twenty years. Directors are convinced that adult film viewers don't care about the male performer as long as he can produce the erection and the money shot. The same seven guys have proved that they can do just that, so they get the work.

Sometimes, though, the opposite problem—too speedy a climax—causes difficulty on the set. Most men want to know how the male stars are able to keep going so long before climaxing. The short answer is, often they don't.

When this happens, the director loops the film so it appears that the act goes on for longer than it actually did. Sometimes this looping is obvious, sometimes you don't really notice it.

Let's face it, close-up shots of two bodies engaging in sex can look very similar. The cheaper companies may even use footage from other movies to loop into a scene.

Wendy McElroy, in her book *XXX: A Woman's Right to Pornography*, relates a discussion she had with John "Buttman" Stagliano and John Leslie on the topic of women's orgasms in adult tapes. Stagliano says 10 to 20 percent of the women's orgasms shown are real, and Leslie says 90 percent are real. Both men agreed that 100 percent of the orgasms in soft erotica are faked.

My estimation for the hard-core productions would have to be closer to Stagliano's 10 percent figure. (To see a real orgasm, go to *Buttman's Rio III* and watch Buttwoman have a zinger in her girl-girl scene.) That's 10 percent *at best*. The percentage in amateur tapes is much higher than that, which is one of the reasons they can be a lot of fun to watch. They're very conscious of this point (in some places too conscious, the men often asking "Didya? Didya?" in excited voices) and do their best to deliver, which is more than the pros often do.

Directors

The director is just as important in an adult film as he or she is in mainstream movies. The indication of quality, though, can not necessarily be judged from a director's name on the box. Many of them do several types of tapes, ranging from sensitive, artistic efforts to the totally barbaric. Use the review section of this book in conjunction with our discussion of various directors' work, and you should be able to make a pick that will please both of you.

Here are some of the directors who usually put out a product that we think will appeal to couples.

Andrew Blake - To paraphrase the old joke about real estate, the top three directors' names in couple's erotica are Andrew Blake, Andrew Blake, and Andrew Blake. Blake, who says he has now quit the business, will appear at the top of the list compiled by anyone who feels they know anything about the couple's market. He is consistently stylish, his performers are almost always fine-looking, and he never attempts to make them act beyond their capabilities. In fact, they seldom even speak.

A criticism sometimes leveled at Blake is that his films lack sexual heat, that he is only interested in presenting artistic photography of women's bodies. While we can understand how those who've watched a lot of these movies might come to feel this way, we don't. It is true that our experience is limited, compared to more professional viewers, and we want to keep it that way. For us, Andrew Blake is a terrific couple's director. We list every one of Blake's films in the review section.

There are other directors, Cameron Grant for one, who are often said to have received the Andrew Blake mantle, but I have yet to find one who can consistently capture the beauty and atmosphere that Blake is able to evoke. See the reviews, see the tapes. You will not be disappointed. Recommended: *Desire, Hidden Obsessions, House of Dreams, Les Femmes Erotiques, Night Trips I* and *II, Secrets,* and *Sensual Exposure.*

The Dark brothers - Usually referred to as the Infamous Dark brothers, we find their tapes too hard-core. They specialize in scenes that focus on women with multiple partners, more than a hint of S&M, unusual body types (the elderly, the obese, dwarves), bizarre story lines, and a general atmosphere of danger. If you want the tough stuff, but done with intelligence, then the Dark brothers are your men. But don't blame us if you're offended. See their *DMJ5: The Inferno* for a representative sample of their work.

Cameron Grant - As noted above, this is the man usually said to be the heir apparent to Andrew Blake. We can see why people say that, but he still doesn't have the master's touch. There's a certain lightness missing, an elegance that just can't be copied. But let's hope he keeps on trying. Recommended: *The Dinner Party, Elements of Desire.*

John Leslie - Leslie said in an interview in a magazine, "One of the reasons porn movies are so boring is that you're just showing pictures of something. You must give them more than pictures." We agree wholeheartedly. Leslie began his career as one of the great performers of the Golden Age. He was good-looking, obviously intelligent, and always reliable. He has carried these characteristics over into his directing career. He has made many excellent films, among those that we have reviewed are *Chameleons, Not the Sequel,* and the more recent *Dog Walker.* He is now also producing a Buttman look-alike series, *The Voyeur,* which we also review. Recommended: *Chameleons, Dog Walker.*

Robert McCallum - One of the Golden Age directors who is still working, though some of his contemporary work consists of uninspired wall-to-wallers, films that have no story or connections and feature one sex act after another. McCallum is still able to make good tapes when he is given the money. Recommended: *Erotika, Exstacy.*

Michael Ninn - Ninn is probably the classiest of the modern directors. His movie *Sex* set the standard for expensive arty erotica in 1995, and in 1996 his *Latex* topped even his earlier effort. Most single-guy viewers consider his films pretentious and arty, which means there is too much story, dialogue, and romance in his work for them. Which is the reason we like him. Ninn is willing to spend money on sets and effects, which inspires his actors and actresses to do their best work. Recommended: *Sex, Sex II, Latex.*

Henri Pachard - Another brilliant Golden Age director who now does mostly wall-to-wallers. His present directing name is Jackson St. Louis, chosen, I assume, because he wants to keep his present work from tainting his good stuff. See his films under the Pachard name, which are story-oriented and very well directed. Skip his St. Louis ones. Recommended: *American Garter, Devil In Miss Jones II.*

Candida Royalle - Royalle is the president and guiding light behind Femme Productions, the company that has as its goal creating films from a woman's perspective and promoting positive sexual role modeling. For a feminist outlook and a soft X, Royalle is the director of choice. She is a former erotic performer and has given other erotica stars a forum as directors in her Star Director series. Recommended: *Christine's Secret, Three Daughters.*

John "Buttman" Stagliano - We discuss Stagliano in the review section under Series Tapes. For the most part he's very good at what he does, but his Buttman tapes just aren't couple's material. He has shown he is an intelligent director with the two *Facedance* tapes and his Buttman stuff can be amusing, but most women don't think that particular series is much of a turn-on. Recommended: *Face Dance I, Face Dance II.*

Paul Thomas - Thomas is a director who can usually be relied upon. Known as a house director for Vivid Video, he has done more of our recommended films than any other director besides Andrew Blake. Thomas has been around since the Golden Age, when he was primarily a performer. He was in the Broadway production of *Hair* and in the movie *Jesus Christ Superstar*, playing the part of the disciple Peter. He was also in stage productions of *Evita* and *Tommy*.

His tapes are considered too story-oriented with too much dialogue by the single-guy type of viewer, but these are just the characteristics that recommend him to us. Some of his efforts are not very good, but many are. And in this business that's a pretty solid recommendation. *Bonnie and Clyde I* and *II, Companion: Aroused 2, The Masseuse II, Sinderella I, The Swap II.*

Chapter 12

Tips for Optimum Viewing

*Y*ou're almost there. You've chosen your tape. Now it's time to play it. After the care you've taken to find the perfect tape, you don't want to lessen the effect by ignoring the romantic environment.

You can't beat a large bed as one of the top-rated places to watch erotic videos. Most homes have televisions in the bedroom, and if the truth be known, many of those sets were bought so that the owners could watch adult videos in bed. But that doesn't mean you should overlook other viewing venues, even though most homes don't have TVs and VCRs in unusual locations.

In other words, the living room couch, floor, easy chair, piano bench, ottoman, card table (be careful!), or any other reasonably comfortable surface can be utilized for someplace a bit unusual.

Many couples have kids. This means a sturdy lock on the bedroom door is a necessity. Just as people may say of their dog, "Oh, he would never bite anyone," many couples say of little Mary or Sam, "He never gets out of bed once we tuck him in." Don't bet on it—in either case.

If you're watching an erotic movie, you're more than likely to be involved in other matters, so you won't hear that telltale click of the door opening and the little voice, "Mom, Dad, what are you doing?"

Don't chance it. A simple latch lock, easily installed, will take out the worry. At least if they have to knock, you're forewarned.

Lighting: Lots of lights, low lights, no lights. Whatever you like. Personally, I find that the shifting colors from the television give me enough light to see, and at the same time masks the inevitable flaws and blemishes on this increasingly worn body. A soft colored night-light is also a good idea. The old scarf over the lamp can also work well, as long as you don't burn down the house in the process. Which is why we gave up using candles after we graduated from college and bought our own house.

And how about wearing some special outfits—faux leopard skin, silk, satin, classy underwear? Sure, why not? Watching these movies will give you lots of ideas in this department. Why not put some of these examples to good use?

The next consideration is the length of the tape and how long you are actually going to watch.

Tapes vary wildly in length. Most boxes will tell you the running time. Amateur tapes are often shorter than professional ones. Some of the tapes are very long, up to four hours. I never really understood why anyone would want a four-hour tape, unless you're buying, in which case you could stretch it out over several months and never repeat a scene. Most of the long ones are orgy tapes.

How long you actually watch the tape will vary, of course. Beth and I find the average time to be twenty to thirty minutes. After all, the purpose of these tapes is to turn you on. And they work. So don't expect to see them all the way through. Some of the better tapes have enough story to keep you interested till the end. In that case, I recommend a multiple rental. Take it out enough times to make it to the end, in two or three or more rentals. Who cares how long it takes?

This can be an advantage if you've bought the film. In fact, it makes buying as cheap as renting in some cases. Cheaper if you buy a tape with more than one film on it.

The Adam and Eve mail-order company offers four Andrew

Blake films, complete, for thirty dollars, plus shipping. See the Resources chapter for their address.

This offer is a real deal. Most couples like Andrew Blake. His films do not have heavy story lines, so there's little reason to watch them all the way through in one sitting. If you break up each film into three or four viewings you've got a minimum of twelve to fifteen sessions. A rental usually goes for three bucks, so you can see the economic advantage of buying. Plus you save a trip to the rental store, and you actually own the tape when you're done watching it. Some couples could stretch a tape like this out over a year.

Pretty cheap entertainment.

(If you've watched, and read, and decided that none of this is for you, and you still want to be turned on as a couple by videocassette, go rent the mainstream Hollywood movie *Don Juan DeMarco*. It's guaranteed to turn on any woman alive. Trust us.)

Chapter 13

So You Wanna Be in Pictures

$\mathcal{N}$ow that you've watched a bunch of these tapes, some of you are going to say, Hey, we can do that! We can be just as good! Let's make our own tape and get rich!

Like most things in life, it's a lot harder than it looks.

If you're going to go pro right off the bat, the largest and most important casting service for erotic actors and actresses is World Modeling Talent Agency, 4523 Van Nuys Boulevard, Van Nuys, CA 91403 (818) 986-4316. If you're a young, beautiful woman, you've got a chance. If you're a guy you don't, unless you can get the young beautiful woman who gets accepted to stipulate she'll only act if you're her partner.

Saying it's a tough business is an understatement of vast proportions. If you're incurably bitten by the bug, better you should stay home and enter on the amateur level.

Start-up on the home level is pretty easy. All you need is a camcorder, a tripod to put it on, and a willing partner. Set the recorder up, point it where you're going to be, and let it roll. After you're finished, play it back, have a few laughs, decide where you could improve, then do it again. If you really get into it, you can get someone to operate the camera while you perform, or you could find some performers and you run the camera.

After you get a decent product you can sell it to one of the amateur companies like Video Alternatives, who puts out a booklet, "Amateur Video Guidelines," that they will send you for free simply for the asking. Further information on Video Alternatives is in the Resources chapter.

Some basic rules you should remember when making your own video: no kids, no animals, no violence, no excretory functions. Don't tape anyone who doesn't know they're being taped and who isn't participating wholeheartedly. If you're into a little friendly bondage, be advised that professionals who make bondage tapes no longer show anyone engaging in sex while using the B&D accoutrements.

Don't play the radio or your favorite CDs for background music—you have to have permission from the people who own the music to do this.

Practice a little with the lights. That overwhelming glare from big lights washes out pale skin until you look about the same shade as the sheets. Enough light, yes, but don't bring in the kliegs.

After watching quite a few amateur videos, we'd like to offer one more tip. Shave. If you're a guy, shave your face. If you're a woman who has decided to go for one of the professional mohawk trims in the nether regions, touch it up before you roll tape. Stubble on anyone, anywhere, makes you look like a bum.

Can you actually make money producing your own videotapes? There's no easy answer to that one, but couples have done so in the past. Video Alternatives accepts materials three different ways: Purchasing the rights to your video outright, licensing it from you and paying royalties, or getting it from you on a wholesale basis if you can dupe enough copies.

Is this *really* possible? Sure is. One of the ways you can tell is by renting or ordering some amateur tapes. To put it charitably, after seeing many of these tapes, an in-shape couple with a modicum of talent could leap right to the forefront of this business. On the average, you get about $1,000 for the rights to an amateur videotape.

Equipment? A Hi-8 camera for under $2,000 is probably your best bet if you can't afford $10,000 for a Betacam SP.

If you want real help in your budding career, the book *Video Sex: How to Capture Your Lovemaking with a Camcorder* by Kevin Campbell has all the information you need. We've seen this book in a national chain bookstore and it is available through the Good Vibrations people. See our Resources chapter for their address.

One last piece of advice: Take off the glasses. It just looks stupid to wear them through the whole thing.

Chapter 14

Resources

Bibliography

These are some books we read while doing our research. We found all of them interesting.

The Good Vibrations Guide to Sex by Cathy Winks and Ann Semans.
  A terrific sex manual with lots of tips and tricks and their own reviews of erotic films.

"The Money Shot" by Susan Faludi, *The New Yorker*, October 30, 1995. This is a fascinating article, must reading for anyone with more than a casual interest in the adult film business.

Raw Talent: The Adult Film Industry as Seen by Its Most Popular Male Star by Jerry Butler. Jerry was a Golden Ager who appeared in many films, then decided he needed to quit the business. He did so, wrote this book, and appeared on numerous talk shows, often with his wife (who played Wednesday on *The Addams Family* television series), taking a position either for or against erotica, depending on how the wind was blowing on that particular day. His book is informative, but most of the performers he talks about are no longer around today, giving the material a very dated feel.

Talk Dirty to Me: An Intimate Philosophy of Sex by Sallie Tisdale. This beautiful little book was one of the first of the feminist tracts to put forth the view that erotica was morally acceptable for modern women to enjoy.

XXX: A Woman's Right to Pornography by Wendy McElroy. An extremely intelligent look at why and how pornography actually benefits women and the feminist movement. If you ever need any ammunition against the forces of censorship and prudery, this is the book that supplies all the answers.

Mail-Order Sources and Interesting Companies

Another way to find the films you're looking for is by sticking with companies that offer what you like. However, since the spectrum of sexual tastes is so broad, most companies have tapes that cross many boundaries—which means that just because you like one tape from a company doesn't mean you'll like all their offerings. As with choosing tapes because of certain favorite directors or performers, sometimes you'll be led astray.

I wrote to many companies and asked them if they had any tapes that they thought would fit into our couple's-market theme. Most didn't respond, some sent tapes, and some called. A few of them understood what we were doing and offered further help in the form of interviews. After some thought, I turned down most offers of extended help, because I felt that if we became too immersed in this world we'd lose our objectivity.

We tabulated which companies' films appeared most often on our best-of list and found that VCA and Vivid were the two most couples friendly. Both companies offer a large selection of shot-on-film videos, and generally you can be assured of a high-quality product. They do produce videos covering the entire spectrum of tastes, so refer to our list or read the box for content.

Adam and Eve - P.O. Box 800, Carrboro, NC 27510, Customer service (919) 929-2147. One of the largest mail-order companies in the U.S., they have a huge selection of videos at reasonable prices plus an extensive line of other sexually oriented material. Many of the films we recommend are in their catalogue. They have the Andrew Blake deal mentioned in chapter 12, the four films (*Night Trips, Night Trips II, Secrets, House of Dreams*) for $39.95, ten bucks per movie, each one of which you'll probably break up into three or four viewings. And you'll own the tape when you're done. An excellent deal.

Avica Entertainment - 9018 Balboa Boulevard, Box 545, Northridge, CA 91325, (800) 992-8422. This is one of the better Pro-Am distributors we've found.

Barely Decent Entertainment - 8231 DeLongpre #1, West Hollywood, CA 90046. This erotica self-help publisher offers the *Porn Star Handbook* for $15.00, with advice on how to break into the erotic video industry.

Blowfish - This is a computer-only resource. They have a strong list of Golden Age films, available for purchase. We don't really agree with many of their recommendations for modern tapes, but they're a great resource for many sexuality areas and addresses on the World Wide Web if you want to further explore the world of erotica. If you have an Internet connection, contact them at http://www.blowfish.com

Bruce Seven Productions - 14141 Covello Street 8C, Van Nuys, CA 91405, (800) 442-6435. This company is comprised of John Leslie Productions and Evil and Elegant Angel Video, and offers some of the more offbeat and fetishistic videos.

Excalibur Films - 3621 W. Commonwealth, Fullerton, CA 92833, (714) 773-5855 or (800) BUY-MOVIES. Excalibur acts as almost a rent-by-mail firm. After buying and viewing their films, you can return them and receive a large discount on subsequent purchases. There are several conditions involved, but this is a very viable method. Free catalogue.

Femme Distributions - 588 Broadway, Suite 1110, New York, NY 10012, (212) 979-5988. Femme has eight tapes for sale and offers a preview tape for $15.00.

Founded in 1984 by ex-adult actress Candida Royalle, Femme Productions pioneered the concept of erotica made by women and intended for women and couples. They have a line of eight films with more in production, all of which are softer than most professional erotica and yet harder than R-rated films from mainstream Hollywood.

Femme is intelligent, and innovative.

Good Vibrations - 1210 Valencia Street, San Francisco, CA 94110, (415) 974-8980. This is another excellent company that is staffed by knowledgeable, friendly helpers who will guide you toward whatever product you are looking for. They stock more than ninety videos, almost every one of them aimed at some area of the women's or couple's market. Their excellent free catalogue is intelligently written and extremely informative.

Reel Life Video - 4032 S. Lamar Boulevard. #500-200, Austin, TX 78704-7900, (512) 444-3762. Another amateur video company. Call for catalogue.

Romantasy - 199 Moulton Street, San Francisco, CA 94123, (415) 673-3137. Romantasy is an erotic boutique started six years ago by Ann Grogan. Ann is, she likes to say, a recovering attorney who decided the hostile environment of the courtroom was not where she wanted to spend her life. After sixteen years of lawyering, the last six with the California attorney general's office, she quit and created Romantasy. Along with their line of sex aids, toys, and implements, Romantasy sells videotapes. They also have a small guide, *Romantasy's Bedside Guide to Video Erotica*, which is excellent, even though we don't agree with some of these choices. Information on catalogues and the guide can be obtained by writing to their Moulton Street address or contacting them via the World Wide Web at http://www. romantasy.com/cyboutique/romantasy

VCA Pictures - 9650 De Soto Avenue, Chatsworth, CA 91311-5012, (800) 421-2386. Big-name professional company with choices that run the gamut from excellent to abysmal. You can't buy direct from them but their product is amply distributed in all stores that carry erotica. If it's a VCA picture you're sure that at least the production values are going to be acceptable. Many of our recommendations are VCA Pictures.

Video Alternatives - 950 Corporate Parkway, Wentzville, MO 63385, (800) 444-8336. This is a mail-order company that specializes in amateur adult erotica. They are extremely nice and helpful. They have three sample tapes that show snippets from the regular line, the samples sell for $20.00 each, and they also will send you a free 42-page catalogue if you call or write. Provide your date of birth on any requests you send them to prove you are of age. They have a super catalogue, the Ultimate Amateur Video Alternatives, that is 300 pages long and lists over 1000 amateur videos. This catalogue is $10 per copy or free with any order of $100. Check them out on the Internet at http://www.videoalt.com.

Video Gold Club - P.O. Box 800, Carrboro, NC 27510, (919) 929-2147. A division of Adam and Eve. Ads for Video Gold Club can often be found in some men's magazines, like *Hustler*. This is a video club that sells you erotic videos the way Book-of-the-Month Club sells you books. In this case, you must buy two tapes in two years at $39.95 each. Which can be a perfectly good deal if you like the tape.

Vivid - 15127 Califa Street, Van Nuys, CA 91411, (800) 423-4227. Another big-name professional production company. They pride themselves on their appeal to couples. They are well represented in all erotic tape outlets, advertising and marketing in all the specialty magazines, and if you call their 800 number they'll send you a free catalogue.

World Modeling - 4523 Van Nuys Boulevard, Suite 203, Sherman Oaks CA 91403, (818) 986-4316. Jim South, a famous name in the erotic video industry, can be contacted regarding modeling for print or video work.

Other Guides

Books

The X-rated Videotape Guide by Robert H. Rimmer. (Covers 1350 films and tapes from 1970–85.) Prometheus Books, 56 John Glenn Drive, Amherst, NY 14228-9826, (800) 421-0351.

The X-rated Videotape Guide II (1200 films and tapes from 1986–1990) Prometheus Books.

The X-rated Videotape Guide III (1990–92) Prometheus Books.

The X-rated Videotape Guide IV by Robert H. Rimmer and Patrick Riley. (1993–94). Prometheus Books.

    The individual books cost $18.95, or a wrapped set of the first three guides is available for $49.95.

The X-rated Videotape Guide and its subsequent editions supply a very short—sometimes only one-or two-sentence—description of over one thousand films in each volume. Generally, the reviews are of the films released during the specific years of each guide. I have seen the books for sale at a chain bookstore, so they are around if you want to take a look at them before buying. The books are useful if you are completely fascinated by the world of adult tapes, or if it's relevant to your job in some way, but as a general guide they don't have much information on which to base a rental or buying decision.

Only the Best by Jim Holliday, 15240 Victory Boulevard #279, Van Nuys, CA 91411. Holliday picks 250 of the best films through 1986. There's plenty of information on the Golden Age films, though it won't do you much good on the more modern films and tapes. Holliday puts out his own line of *Only the Best* videos, see review section.

Magazines

Adult Video News Buyer's Guide—This is a monthly magazine that has reviews and pictures and stories about the people who put out these tapes. It's aimed at the buyers who choose tapes for rental stores, but it makes an interesting read for the layperson. Lots of flashy ads for upcoming tapes. An annual subscription is $44.95, and single copies are $4.95. I've seen it for sale in adult bookstores and even on the rack at Tower Records, so it's available if you look for it.

For $10.95, they put out an annual list of the year's best tapes. This is a useful guide as long as you are aware that their position on the tapes comes from a business standpoint, not a consumer's.

Adam Film World and Adult Video Guide—This is another monthly magazine devoted to the world of adult video. It's a lot more hard-core than the previous listing and sells for $4.95 an issue. They also have a very useful year-end compendium of the best videos, including many amateur videos. They also list retail sources for tapes by state, plus a source directory by company, almost all of which sell tapes via mail order. If you're having trouble finding tapes, this magazine can help you locate them. Available at your standard adult-magazine store, or by mail at 8060 Melrose Avenue, Los Angeles, CA 90046-7082. If you *still* are having trouble finding videos, write to their Reader Service Department, *Adam Film World Guide*, 8060 Melrose Avenue, Los Angeles, CA 90046-7082.

Include a SASE with your name, address, and age verification, and they'll help you out.

Hustler Erotic Video Guide—$4.95 for monthly issue. More hardcore than either of the above mags, it can often be amusing to read, especially the columns. But the reviews primarily reflect a single-male viewpoint.

If you've ever read any sexually oriented magazines, you've seen ads telling you that you can buy hundreds of movies for only a few bucks. Don't bother. Like anything else for sale, you've got to figure you're going to get what you pay for. What you receive are hundreds of scenes, not movies, and the scenes are edited so that some of them are only a few seconds long. These scenes are packed onto a single tape and recorded at extended play, the slowest recording speed possible, which gives you horrendous tracking problems. Don't waste your money.

Internet Erotica Information

Before I decided to write this book, I surfed the Web and found lots of sex-related sites. Many had to do with erotic videos. Chief among them is the web site for the alt.sex.movies group (http://home.eznet.net/~rwillhelm/asm). Here I found all the experts I could ever want. My immediate thought was to contact these people and solicit help. But the more I read, the more I realized it was not a good idea.

The ASM folks are intelligent, funny, and really know the business. Viewing these tapes is a labor of love for them, and they see plenty of them. It seemed to me, after lurking in the background and reading their posts, that they knew too much for our purposes. If you work at an ice cream factory you might not get sick of ice cream, but you get desensitized to the real pleasures of the every-once-in-a-while ice cream cone. No matter what you do, it changes from the treat that it once was. It can still be a pleasure, but not a special treat.

The people at ASM are the people down at the ice cream

factory. Their tastes, for the most part, seemed more rarefied, a little more extreme for having been involved in this particular world more than my wife and myself. So I didn't talk to any of these professionals; I lurked and listened and read, and I learned. I recommend their Websites as must reading for anyone who wants a more in-depth look than we've given here.

Our reviews are different than theirs. We were offended by some things they found quite acceptable, and we were not bothered or bored by some things they found all too tame and predictable. It isn't a matter of being right or wrong, merely a matter of proximity: They're a lot closer to this world than we are. We each see differently from our own vantage point.

So to the Imperator, and the Director, and Peter, and Jaguar Night, and all the other experts at ASM, thanks for teaching us, even if you didn't know we were in the audience.

We decided not to include addresses for Internet erotica sites, as Web pages are extremely transitory. The ASM has been a constant presence on the Net for several years and seems likely to remain so. Check it out for further research and enjoyment. Any search engine can locate erotica-oriented sites by searching the word *sex*.

Part Two

Reviews

*O*ur review section is a little different from most. We decided to skip the usual rating method because we wanted to give you only good choices. No four stars, no smiley faces, no partial to fully erect penises, no complicated systems. We've included a few that we think you should stay away from, for various reasons, but the rest of them are all good. We've tried to make our reasons for liking the tapes clear, so you can apply your own tastes against ours and come to an understanding of the review and choose an enjoyable film. And as you watch more tapes, you will begin to recognize the performers, producers, and directors who most appeal to you. To help you we have included in each review the name at the production company, the director, and the cast, as well as a synopsis and our opinion.

At the expense of sounding stuffy, we have to say that there is no personal judgment that can encompass all tastes, nor any real standard that takes into account differing personalities. Sexual preferences in particular are difficult to predict. It is not our business or choice to dictate to your sexuality. And yet we think we can suggest possibilities that exist within certain parameters of intelligence and good taste.

Though there may not be something on our review list for absolutely everyone, there is certainly something for most people. We feel that we're presenting tapes that have couple's appeal. That doesn't mean you won't enjoy them if you watch them alone, or that you won't find some good tips if you aren't part of a couple. And some of them may even offend you, but we hope we've clearly indicated those that might.

Almost all the tapes were rented from several local mom-and-pop–type video stores. We had to get some of the tapes recommended by various people from distributors, but for the most part all of the reviewed offerings are easily available in stores. If you can't find them as rentals, they're available through the mail-order services listed in the Resources chapter.

We couldn't possibly have watched each and every video as a couple—there were just too many of them and the wife-half of the couple has a regular job she has to get up for every day. All films were watched all the way through to make sure there were no untoward surprises. But thank God for the fast-forward button.

We thought we would become bored after a while, but after watching hundreds of these tapes they still retained that magical, aphrodisiac ability that they possessed from the very beginning. Amazing.

Remember, we're just regular people. We're not experts on film or eroticism or sexuality. I'm sure that there are many out there who could give you more expert advice, more information, and more astute opinions. That's not the point. We just want to steer you toward tapes that we think you'll like.

Chapter 1

Easy Does It: Soft Core

Soft-core erotica is more fully examined in the early chapters of this book. Our conclusion: It's an excellent starting point for adult-oriented viewing. These are some of our favorites.

THE RED SHOE DIARIES

Saunders/King productions. DIRECTOR: *Zalman King.* CAST: *David Duchovny, Brigitte Bako, Billy Wirth, Kai Wulff, Bridget Ryan, Evie Sullivan, Brenda Vaccaro*

The Red Shoe Diaries was one of the first of the nonrated or NC-17 movies to tap into mainstream America's hunger for sex on videotape. This title began as a series on cable television and has now spun off into direct-to-video tapes. Because the first tape is the pilot for the others, we'll deal with it at length.

The film opens on a graveyard scene, featuring David Duchovny—who is in all of the *Red Shoe* movies, though he's gone on to become famous as FBI agent Fox Mulder on television's *The X-Files*—mourning at the grave of his girlfriend, Alex, played by the lovely Brigitte Bako. He goes home to his fabulous Manhattan loft where they once lived. As he's cleaning out her closet, he stumbles across her diary. He sits down and begins to read.

It seems that Alex had been leading a double life.

She begins, in voice-over, to talk about her relationship with her boyfriend, Jake (Duchovny). He's a successful architect, she's an interior designer. They live in his incredible loft: huge, with large models of his buildings, spotlights, a fireplace, park bench, bar, basketball court, and I don't know what else.

She loves Jake, she says in the diary, but she's bothered because it is all *too* perfect. She feels herself to be deeply flawed.

She's walking along one day after a minor eye operation and she literally runs into a construction worker, played by Billy Wirth. This guy is terrific looking, with lots of muscles and that construction worker joie de vivre. They chat for a minute, he goes back to work with his jackhammer and hits a water main. Whoosh! The water spurts skyward. Subtle use of imagery.

Alex is very turned on by the guy.

Beth, the other half of the reviewing team, was also very turned on by the guy. And, I have to admit, I could see why. This scene is essentially the model for the now-famous commercial where the women all go to the window and watch the construction worker take off his shirt and drink a diet Coke. Except the guy in *Red Shoe* is even better looking.

A few days later Alex goes back to the construction site, locates the guy, and follows him. She finds he works part-time in a shoe shop. She goes in and he sells her a pair of very high-heeled, very sexy, red shoes. He's got some rough edges, unlike her boyfriend, but he strokes her leg and talks a little dirty to her and she likes that. He gives her his home address and tells her to be there day after tomorrow at eight o'clock.

Against her better judgment, but drawn by her rebellion against her perfect life, she goes. He lives in a fairly ratty little house on the bad side of town. They have a few minutes of verbal jousting, then they have sex. Without being particularly explicit, this scene is sexier than most see-all scenes in adult video. It is fast, hard, and beautifully edited.

One of the main points of this movie—who shall have control

in a relationship—is graphically made in this scene. At first, the construction worker demands control, in rather crude ways. "Get down on your knees," he commands. But Alex not only rejects this approach, she seizes control and dominates the lovemaking. The man and the woman literally wrestle with each other for supreme position in the relationship.

Alex's fascination with the man, whose name turns out to be Tom, lies in a favorite fantasy for women as well as men: rough, anonymous sex with a beautiful partner. Alex sums it up in one of her diary entries: "He makes love like he worked on the street. Tender as a jackhammer." Afterward, Alex goes back to her perfect existence. Her boyfriend Jake asks her to marry him. Meanwhile, Tom hunts her down.

There is a stalker element to this video, but it is not as crudely delineated as in most mainstream films or movies-of-the-week. Alex actually initiates the affair by following Tom to the shoe store. When she then tries to end it (not very convincingly) and Tom refuses to take her *no* seriously, it's difficult to feel sorry for Alex. Especially when it's obvious to the viewer *and* Tom that she loves having sex with him.

Jake presses her to marry, Tom refuses to let her go. Alex, who has given us a glimpse of her troubled psyche, cannot deal with the situation. She kills herself.

The flashback of Jake reading the diary has now caught up with the movie. We move ahead in the present day.

Jake decides to find Tom. He locates the shoe store and asks to buy a pair of red shoes for his girlfriend. They're all out of red shoes. Later, Jake follows Tom to a bar and engages him in conversation. They are joined by some ladies and retire to Jake's loft to play basketball. Yes, I know it sounds stupid, but this one-on-one basketball game between the shirtless Jake and Tom is the pivotal point of the movie, breathtaking because you can't anticipate the outcome: Will Jake try to kill Tom? That certainly seems his intent. Will Tom figure out what is going on? Not until Jake tells him who he really is. Rent the tape to find the answer to these questions.

The movie ends with Jake, in an odd restaurant/post office

kind of place, writing on a piece of paper. He goes outside and uses a pay phone to place an ad in a newspaper.

"Have you been betrayed?" he asks in his ad. "Have you kept a diary?" He says he will pay money for stories and diaries sent to him.

Thus initiating the series of films to follow.

I have gone on at some length with this film to set up the ones that come after. Their reviews will be shorter. Much to our surprise, Beth and I both liked this movie, and think it is an excellent starting point for erotic film viewing. If you're already beyond this level, leap ahead to the more hard-core tapes. But even for the viewers used to seeing their sex bold and explicit, this film has a lot to offer.

RED SHOE DIARIES 2: DOUBLE DARE

Saunders/King productions DIRECTOR: *Zalman King, Tibor Takaas.*
CAST: *Steven Bauer, Joan Severance, Denise Crosby, Robert Knepper, Laura Johnson, Arnold Vosloo, Michael Woods, David Duchovny*

The second installment in the series differs from the first in that instead of one long story, it is made up of three shorter, independent stories. On the whole, this tape is sexier than the original as far as the graphic sexual elements, but we only really liked one of the three segments.

The first story is our favorite. It is introduced by Duchovny in the usual way: He goes to the restaurant/post office, gets his mail, then sits outside and reads it to his faithful dog. The letter's content dissolves into screen action.

A beautiful lady is trying to hail a taxi in a pouring rainstorm. She's drenched. A cab stops and a good-looking man offers to share the cab with her. She demurs at first, but eventually gets in. He convinces her to borrow his sportcoat, then to take off her blouse so she won't freeze, then to come up to his place for a cup of soup. All of the foregoing is accomplished only by much entreaty. It's annoying because we know she'll eventually do all of it, but we're sympathetic because we know, along with the lady, that it's not really a good idea to accept such kindnesses from strangers. Even good-looking ones.

They go to his palatial loft and make love on the floor. She (no names are given) is a wonderfully beautiful Sophia Loren look-alike, and there are plenty of full-body nude shots. Tastefully done, of course, remember this is still soft-core.

The two of them decide to become Tuesday and Thursday lovers, the ultimate safe sex: unencumbered, unentangled, and anonymous. Each time they meet they make a special effort to engage in unusual and interesting activity. All of these sex scenes are beautifully photographed.

Her brother dies, she goes to her lover for comfort, she snoops in his mail and learns his name. He says she's broken the rules. While she's out of town for the brother's funeral, he moves away. When she comes back, she goes to his old address and can't find him. He eventually comes back and says he wants to have a normal relationship. She agrees.

I hope I haven't ruined the suspense for anyone with this bare-bones synopsis, but suspense really isn't the point with these tapes. The sequence continues the theme of who's in control in a relationship. It's all very lovely and erotic to look at, the people are beautiful, the photography perfect, and the production lush. Which is the reason we like the *Diaries* in the first place.

The second sequence is about a lady cop who kidnaps a man she takes a liking to, handcuffs him to a chair, and then over several hours convinces him that such tactics are a perfectly reasonable way to get a date. I thought the woman cop looked like a demented Glenn Close, and nothing about being kidnapped and handcuffed to a chair seemed even faintly erotic to me. At least as presented by this lady. She raves on about control, the overriding theme of the *Diaries*. She tells us her daddy always said, "Play to win. Never give up control." Bzzzzzzz. Fast forward.

The last sequence was more fun, but it still couldn't match the first.

Here we have an attractive lady who works in advertising. She works late at night and notices a great-looking guy in an office in the building across the street. She's married but decides, as do all the women in the *Diaries*, to have a fling. Or a semi-fling, at least.

This is a standard erotica story, but with a nineties twist. She waves at the guy, then he somehow figures out her fax number, so they begin faxing dares back and forth: Dare you to take off your shirt, double-dare you to take off you blouse, etc.

Every night the lady goes home and works off her accumulated sexual tension on her husband, who doesn't know what is going on but is grateful for what he's getting. After much back-and-forth, the woman and her across-the-street lover meet and he asks her to make love in the back seat of his car. She turns him down.

In the end she wonders if she's been unfaithful. It's a thorny philosophical question, one that we were unable to answer. Each viewer will have to decide for him or herself. Or you can do what we did instead of wrestling with such weighty issues: Rewind the tape and watch the first story again. It's worth the rental, even if you decide to skip the rest.

RED SHOE DIARIES 4: AUTO EROTICA

Saunders/King productions DIRECTOR: *Zalman King.* CAST: *Ally Sheedy, Scott Plank, Marina Giulia Cavalli, Nicholas Chinlund, Caitlin Dulany, Sheryl Lee, David Duchovny*

The first of the three vignettes in this tape is a lightweight sex comedy. Ally Sheedy's character and her husband lead an active sex life based primarily on videotaping themselves as they have sex while Sheedy wears sexy lingerie and wigs. Nothing very kinky for this pair.

Their live-in Italian maid finds the clothing, dresses up, beckons the pool boy, and lies down to wait. Hubby comes home early, goes to the bedroom, sees what he thinks is his wife (from the back), and slips up behind her and makes love to her. Halfway through, the wig comes off and both are shocked to find the mistake that has been made. Believable? No. But who cares? The taping system is on and this encounter is recorded.

Sheedy comes home, slips into her outfit, puts on a videotape, and is horrified to see her husband making love to the maid. Much shouting ensues. Eventually everything is straightened out, the maid gets the pool boy, the rich couple are content with each other, the vignette is over.

If you're an Ally Sheedy fan, you could watch it. If you're not, you could easily FF through this one.

Vignette two is the Auto Erotica of the title. A beautiful woman is driving a red Corvette and a good-looking guy in a blue car challenges her to a race. They drive wildly over winding roads, through tunnels, up and down mountains. It is the director's intent to make beautiful people driving beautiful cars in a crazed manner sexy.

It works.

During the course of the race we learn that the woman is on her way to her own wedding rehearsal.

The two cars end up in the desert in a surreal location where seemingly hundreds of jumbo jet airplanes are being stored. The woman grabs the man's car key and throws it into the desert. After she tells the man she does not wish to know his name, that she has thrown his key away to insure that he will not follow her, they make love on top of one of the cars. They have sex the way they drive, fast and hard.

Then it's over.

I liked it. So did Beth. We're thinking about buying a Corvette.

The third vignette involves the star of the series, Jake, played by David Duchovny. He meets a beautiful blond photographer. By now we hope that Jake will finally find a soul mate to match the dead Alex from *Diaries 1*, so we're rooting for him.

He and the photographer spar verbally for a while, then she

takes him along on a photo shoot. They go to a trailer where she photographs a tattooed man making love with an Asian woman. This is filmed very erotically, much slower than the slam-bam sex of the Auto Erotica segment.

The photographer and Jake go back to her place and make love. Afterward, she invites him to a show of her photographs. Jake goes to the gallery, looks at her pictures, and then, for some reason we really didn't understand, she dumps him. He's back on his own—well, not exactly on his own, he still has his faithful dog—and the series goes on.

Putting aside the comedic first vignette, the second and third continue the *Red Shoes* theme: In sexual situations, the power belongs to women. They control whether or not the act will occur. Once the act has occurred, they have the power to end the relationship. These women choose to have sex with no entanglements, either anonymously or nearly so.

Zalman King, the director and producer, seems to think this is sexy.

He's right.

PENTHOUSE LETTERS: VOLUME II

I once had a friend who worked in the letter department at *Penthouse*. When I asked if those wacky letters were written by the editors themselves, my friend said absolutely not, they're all real. They may have been the product of some pretty fevered imaginations, but they were all sent in by outsiders.

What *Penthouse* has done here is taken the letters and used them for mini screenplays. There are several tapes in this series, and probably more to come. They were all pretty much alike so *Volume II* will suffice as representative. Each tape is a series of vignettes. This one had all the standards: the randy nurse, the broken-down car where the man is "rescued" by a lovely woman who has sex with him in the back seat, the two girls in the hot tub joined by two stud-muffins, etc.

This is pretty formulaic in many ways, but it's always done with a sense of humor. The participants are very good-looking, and while the sex is simulated, it can be stimulating. What we have here is the moving-picture version of *Penthouse* magazine. More explicit than *Playboy*, but nothing really hard-core. Nice light fodder for a beginner's evening. We could see putting these tapes on at a party and giving people some laughs, adding a light tone of sexuality, and not offending anyone. Sounds pretty good to us.

Chapter 2

Ladies Night: Mostly Femme Films

I like my erotic videos to be more hard-core than Beth usually prefers, so it was with some reluctance that I approached Candida Royalle's Femme series of tapes aimed at the feminine side of the couple's market. Shame on me for being so close-minded and pretentious. Some of this series is among the best on the shelves.

Femme directors never show the extreme anatomical close-ups so beloved of the hard-core crowd, but the Femme tapes contain the same sexy lovemaking as raunchier videos. A strong emphasis on story also buoys these tapes far above many in the adult mainstream crowd.

FEMME: CHRISTINE'S SECRET

DIRECTORS: *Candida Royalle and R. Lauren Neime.* CAST: *Carol Cross, Jake West, Chelsea Blake, George Payne, Tajia Rae, Joey Silvera, Marita Ekberg, Anthony Casino*

Christine's Secret is a fine example of a Femme tape. Although I thought it somewhat skimpy on story and with a plain-Jane cast,

I agree with Beth that its greatest appeal lies in the male performances.

The film takes place at a country bed-and-breakfast where Carol Cross has come to stay for the weekend. There she sees the other guests and staff in sexual situations, but remains personally unfulfilled. In the first scene, she masturbates while a young man watches and does the same. A second scene between the husband-and-wife owners of the B&B is very erotic—the first of several stellar male performances. A third encounter has veterans Tajia Rae and Joey Silvera in the barn for some spirited lovemaking, and a newlywed couple go at it in their bedroom. Carol Cross pleasures herself on different occasions throughout the film. The final scene is the pinnacle of eroticism: a long, slow, dreamy sequence with Carol joined by the young man of her fantasies. Beth liked the natural lighting of the scene and thought it was romantic and sexy. I resolved to emulate some of the actor's moves.

This tape is long on fantasy and features a good-looking, accomplished male cast. The women were not as attractive, but they gave as good as they got in the sexual scenes, so I found the film quite arousing. Anyone, not just women, should enjoy the combination of beautiful pastoral setting, handsome enthusiastic actors, and vigorous sensual lovemaking.

FEMME: REVELATIONS

DIRECTOR: *Candida Royalle*. CAST: *Amy J. Rapp, Colin Mathews, Martin and Nicole London, Ava Grace, Paris Phillips, Michele Capozzi*

This film is presented as the crown jewel in the Femme collection, their first effort to be filmed in 35mm, rather than on videotape.

The story is set in a violently repressive future where sex is forbidden, unless it is for procreative purposes. The lead actress, Amy Rapp, is married to a fellow who takes the dictates of the state very seriously. Amy gets no sexual pleasure from this robotic lover.

One day, after their unconventional neighbor is dragged off by black-uniformed goons, Amy discovers a secret room in his now-empty apartment. In this room is a television set and videotapes, which turn out to be of people having sex, obviously for pleasure. Amy watches these tapes and masturbates, a theme that makes up most of the film. She eventually gets herself in trouble, which we know must happen from the very beginning, and in the end she is hauled off to some unknown fate.

First of all, it must be said that high ideals and feminist convictions do not themselves make a better or more well-acted plot. The chief problem with this film, at least as far as we were concerned, is that while it was generally tasteful, there was no real "heat" generated, except in the last, lesbian scene. And even there, only one of the two women appeared to climax—and it must be remembered that women having orgasms is one of the hallmarks of a Femme film.

Revelations fulfills all the criteria of the feminist erotic film, but still, in the end, we thought it was boring, proving that even in the world of politically correct sexuality, good intentions are not necessarily enough.

FEMME: RITES OF PASSION

Rites of Passion is one of the two Femme Star Director Series, short films directed by women who were and sometimes still are mainstream adult actresses. There are two stories in each tape, and each story is approximately forty minutes long.

RITES OF PASSION:
IN SEARCH OF THE ULTIMATE SEXUAL
EXPERIENCE

DIRECTOR: *Annie Sprinkle.*   CAST: *Jeanna Fine, Rodger T. Dodger, David Sandler*

This is an autobiographical story from Annie Sprinkle, a veteran adult performer.

Jeanna Fine, in voice over, recounts how she has tried everything searching for the ultimate sexual experience. She's experimented with all the known variations, she's done it all. One night she picks up a bodybuilder and takes him home. She dumps out a truckload of sex toys and they begin making love. Partway through, she realizes she's bored. The bodybuilder is performing, but she decides that the whole thing is a waste of time and kicks him out.

Suddenly, a genie appears magically in front of her. He, it turns out, is her spirit guide. He does gymnastic tricks, explains the secrets of tantric love, and turns her on to health food. They make long, slow love.

Not only an apt pupil, Jeanna takes the lessons to heart, finds the bodybuilder again, and teaches him the techniques she has learned.

An epigraph in the credits after the story ends says:

"It is time to remember sex as being the truly sacred act that it is . . . a deep meditation, a dance of the forces of creation."
—Marcus Allen, *Tantra for the West*

Good advice for everyone.

RITES OF PASSION:
SHADY MADONNA

DIRECTOR: *Veronica Vera.*   CAST: *Nina Hartley, Robert Bullock, Scott Baker*

Mr. Morality (Scott Baker) is meeting with the station manager of KFEM-TV. He's there to tape one of his fire-and-brimstone sermons warning viewers of the dangers of sin. The station receptionist sits him in the lobby to wait, where he falls asleep.

He dreams that the receptionist, now wearing a short skirt and exposing her breasts, is enticing him to have sex. Mr. Morality gives his sermon against sin. He wakes up and goes to lunch.

The receptionist and the station manager, on a whim, decide to have sex on-camera. Mr. Morality comes back from lunch, sees this, and eventually joins in.

He wakes up, realizes it was all a dream, and runs out.

Both of these vignettes were kind of cute, but nothing you could call particularly steamy. It's a nice idea to have women erotica stars as directors, but we can't really say that their day jobs have made them any better, or given them more insight into the making of an erotic tape.

FEMME: A TASTE OF AMBROSIA

A Taste of Ambrosia is the second of the Femme Star Director Series, where women adult erotica stars are given the opportunity to make their own sexy tapes. Again, two short vignettes:

A TASTE OF AMBROSIA: NINE LIVES HAVE MY LOVE

DIRECTOR: *Candida Royalle.*   CAST: *Jeanna Fine, Rugby Rhodes*

Jeanna is an artist who loves her two cats. Her boyfriend, though, accuses her of loving the cats more than him. The boyfriend is a likable guy, but his insistence on the cat thing really begins to get to Jeanna. On top of this, with his constant hanging around he is getting in the way of her work for a show of her paintings.

She entices the boyfriend to pose in the nude for her, then makes love to him. In the end, she has turned him into a cat, just as she did to her two former boyfriends.

A Taste of Ambrosia:
The Pick Up

DIRECTOR: *Veronica Hart.*   CAST: *Alexis Firestone, Randy Paul*

A typical suburban mom, dressed in sweatsuit, looks at her watch and realizes she is going to be late. She takes a bath. Cut to a man at a desk who looks at his watch and realizes he is also going to be late. He takes a shower.

The camera cuts back and forth between these two people. There is no dialogue.

We next see the woman, dressed in a fancy hooker outfit, on a street corner talking to a guy. The man who took the shower comes up to her, picks her up, and takes her back to his place. They undress each other, she puts a bright green condom on him, they make love.

It turns out that they're really man and wife. Grandma is there to take care of the kids and they staged the routine to spice up their love life.

What a surprise!

This particular series of Femme tapes, the Star Director Series, is pretty sleepy if you're into any of the more hard-core stuff. Of the two stories in *Ambrosia* we found *Nine Lives* better. The cat story rings pretty true to your average male, who has probably been involved with at least one cat-woman in his life.

In both *Passion* and *Ambrosia*, the women are quite attractive, and all have natural, implant-free bodies. This natural breast thing, actually, is getting to be a real turn-on, the exact opposite of what mainstream adult film makers think.

The sex isn't exactly steamy, but these are fine starter tapes. They have all the proper Femme credentials, and nothing in them will shock or repulse. We liked some of the other Femme tapes better, but these are short and kind of cute.

FEMME: THREE DAUGHTERS

DIRECTOR: *Candida Royalle.* CAST: *Siobhan Hunter, Gloria Leonard, Robert Bullock, Carol Cross, Nina Preta, Annette Heinz, Johnny Nineteen, Ashley Moore, Clark Sharp*

A quick glance at the cast of performers will show that the only really recognizable name is Gloria Leonard. This is a plus. None of the usual faces and bodies. All of these people are attractive and real looking. It's a pleasure to see them.

We liked this early effort by Ms. Royalle better than her much-heralded 35mm effort, *Revelations*, reviewed above. It's the story of a family reunion that takes place over spring break, when all three daughters are home for a few days. Mom, played by veteran erotic actress Gloria Leonard, is the best actor in the bunch, though the others are at least adequate. The three daughters are a concert pianist, a career woman home from her job in London, and the eighteen-year-old who is soon to graduate from high school.

The action centers around the youngest, who watches her sisters interact with their lovers and dreams of her own sexual awakening. An early scene features Betty Dodson's book on self-loving. (See review on pages 95–96.)

The pianist gets it on with her priggish teacher on the living-room floor, the career woman accepts her boyfriend's proposal and makes love in her bedroom, and yes, the young girl finally snags a good-looking guy and learns the beauty of physical love.

And mom and dad have an interlude in the attic.

All the sex is graphic, although the gynecological close-ups are omitted. There are no external ejaculations, no facials, none of the standard money shots that are mandatory in most of mainstream erotica. And the eroticism of the sex scenes suffer not one bit for the loss.

Beth and I both liked this tape. We can quibble with some of the production: The taped-on-location sound is not great, often the actors emote like collegiate thespians, and the career daughter goes a little too far in her protestations of love, but these are minor faults. If you like soap operas, or at least don't mind them, this is a fine tape. And besides, the house where it was shot looks like a nice place to live, rather than the glitzy porn-producer palaces we usually see in hard-core productions. Homey—sort of like the tape itself.

We feel that anyone—men, women, or couples—who is interested in erotic films should take the opportunity for a Femme rental, but for a purchase you should review the story and cast of every offering to make sure you get what you want.

As starter films, and for those whose political considerations and credentials are particularly important, the Femme films certainly have their place. We can only hope that in the future Femme films will continue their direction, but will produce films that are as stimulating as many of their counterparts in the conventional erotic film market, and in fact are as stimulating as some of their other tapes.

CABIN FEVER

DIRECTOR: *Deborah Shames*.   CAST: *Belinda Farrell, Judd Dunning*

This is not a Femme-produced tape, but we have included it in this section because it follows the same woman-oriented principles. It's a 45-minute tape that you're probably not going to find for rent in video stores, but rather for purchase through catalogues.

Belinda is a fortyish woman, an artist, alone in a house where she is working on her paintings. Occasionally she gets a call from her daughter who asks how things are going. The impression is the woman has come here to work, away from the pressures of home. We are also led to understand that there is no husband. Belinda is attractive, and appears to have had a very well done breast augmentation.

Enter Judd, the handyman, who has been sent to fix things up around the house. He's a good-looking hunk, and Belinda takes an immediate dislike to him, even though she is obviously intrigued by his looks.

Sound familiar? This is the stuff of many mainstream erotic tapes, but here the plot has been moved to higher planes, the characters (and subsequently the audience) are treated with more intelligence.

Judd sets up his boom box and goes to work. Instead of Vince Gill or the Smashing Pumpkins, we get Mahler and Beethoven. He comes into the living room and makes astute observations about Belinda's art.

Belinda is attracted, but fights her urges. Then, on a dark and stormy night, she gets a cold. She's running a fever. She sits in front of the fire, thinks about her handyman, and pleasures herself. She has a real honest-to-goodness orgasm. Judd comes in (after the orgasm), sees that she's ill, draws her a hot bath, cooks soup, lights candles, washes her back, and they make love on the big old four-poster bed.

The next morning she wakes up and he's gone. She goes about her painting, but longs for Judd. Eventually he shows up and everything is right with the world again.

I thought for sure that Beth was going to like this one.

She didn't.

"The people are too ordinary-looking," Beth says. She thought Belinda was kind of over-the-hill.

Never mind Beth, I thought this tape would be great if you had a woman friend who had just gone through a divorce or had been dating and still not found a soul mate—you'd buy this tape and send it to her and tell her to send it to someone else when she was finished. Someone else who needed cheering up. Besides, I get tired of the guys having all the orgasms. Sure, it's formulaic and soap operaish, but it's also romantic and not really long enough to get tedious.

Like I said, buy it and send it to a woman friend who needs a lift.

Chapter 3

How To:
The Teaching Tapes

NINA HARTLEY'S GUIDE TO BETTER FELLATIO
NINA HARTLEY'S GUIDE TO BETTER CUNNILINGUS

Adam & Eve. PRODUCED AND DIRECTED BY *Nina Hartley*

These two videos feature erotic film star Nina Hartley guiding the viewer through the best techniques for oral sex. As Nina is (no, really) a registered nurse, she can certainly handle the anatomical terminology, close-up slide show, and biological charts she uses to illustrate male and female genitalia. However, in terms of heat, these tapes fall short of the mark. The tapes suffer from a wealth of medical descriptions and clinical detail about the inner workings of the penis and vagina. Knowing about the pubo coccygeus or the corpus cavernosum hasn't altered our present techniques appreciably.

We did learn one Fun Fact To Know And Tell—eating celery will make your semen taste sweet. Nina gives good head to Alex Sanders, but pauses every few moments to describe what she's doing, and some guy named Moose services Angela Faith. I couldn't see that he did anything extraordinary, although Angela praised his technique.

Each tape ends with a fantasy sequence. The cunnilingus tape fares much better, as the instructional portion of the tape is short and most of the video is the fantasy. Beth and I both tried a couple of moves from these tapes, with satisfying results, but Nina's best advice on both videos is to listen to your partner, and do what they tell you. If your lover is woefully inadequate at satisfying you orally, these tapes are a useful guide, but the best advice, as always, comes from within.

PENTHOUSE:
KAMA SUTRA, THE ART OF MAKING LOVE

This one is a keeper. After years of intermittent puzzling over various editions of the Kama Sutra, I watched this tape and now I understand. The four performers involved are all really good-looking and there is clear, intelligently written narration from Indra Sinha. And fine direction from Nick Jones.

Just let me list the names of some of the positions demonstrated, and a couple of the tips: The Eight Kinds of Cunnilingus, The Eight Kinds of Fellatio, Flicking the Tip, Stripping the Mango, The Sporting of Swans, The Turnaround, The Bull, The Sky Foot, The Swing, The Lovemaking of the Crow, The Widely Yawning, Sweet Love, The Rising, The Squeeze.

"Whatever you are doing, slow down—it will be twice as good at half speed."

"Once passion is stirring, lovers should bring their fingernails into play."

There's a special section on sex on a table, and a special section on sex in the garden. They even tell you what flowers to plant.

I've already ordered my own personal copy.

PLAYBOY'S EROTIC WEEKEND GETAWAYS

This tape offers five sensual vignettes of lovers in exotic places: a snowy mountain cabin, a remote desert, a spa, the beach, and even one's own bedroom. More than a travelogue, *Playboy's Erotic Weekend Getaways* gives you the impetus to get away together, and the blueprint of happiness for when you do.

You might have the impression that you will be told of a specific place for a sexy vacation, say Cancun, Mexico, or Vail, Colorado. Rather than providing exact locations, the purpose here is to show *how* to have an erotic weekend getaway, not merely *where*. The idea is to escape from the routine and bring back some of the excitement and freshness to your relationship. Forget about work, the kids, the fast breakaway of everyday life. Concentrate on the special person in your life for two days. And not just the weekend that falls on your paid work vacation, but any of the fifty-two during the year.

The narration and visuals provide suggestions on how to please each other—breakfast in bed, bathing together, reading to your lover, massages, role-playing—that at first glance seem obvious, but, really, how many of us do these things? Particularly on a vacation, when we're usually trying to get the most for our money. Emulating anything featured here, be it licking honey from your lover's shoulder or putting satin sheets on the bed, will almost certainly lead to even more interesting situations.

As with any Playboy video, the cinematography is impeccable and the setting and performers beautiful. Though the vignettes are undeniably tamer than even a soft-core film, they are very romantic and help create a more sensuous mood than the standard in-your-face screwing. The slower pace also emphasizes that we can take our time with sex. After viewing this video, you're not so crazed with lust that you can't enjoy a slower, lazier, more relaxed session of lovemaking.

If it inspires you to take off for the weekend and pamper yourselves, great. That's the point. If you can't afford to get away, that's all right too. The video only costs you a couple of bucks and you can always pretend.

PLAYBOY: MAKING LOVE SERIES, VOL. II
TANTRIC LOVEMAKING

This is one of the instructional tapes from *Playboy*, from the *Making Love* series. We chose this one because it's the one they had for rent at our local video store and it fit with our goal of learning all about various exotic Oriental and Indian techniques. *Playboy* carries the whole line for purchase.

Various instructors tell you how to make your love life better. In this tape, sexologist Dr. Barbara Keesling promises to spice up your sex life with an infusion of Tantric techniques.

Dr. Keesling is an attractive lady with a good body. The surprise element in this how-to tape is that the good doctor gets naked right along with the students. She doesn't exactly join in the action, but she talks them through the techniques and occasionally moves a hand into a better position. This is some bedside manner.

The tape is shot with handsome people and through a gauzy lens. There's an occasional flash of a penis, never erect, and full frontal nudity from the beautiful ladies. The sex is obviously fake, but there's nothing unattractive about any of it.

Here we learned about breathing, massage, playing with paintbrushes, love points, and various positions.

We picked up a few tips, I have to admit. Did you know that there are nerves that connect the nipples, clitoris, and that little place on a woman's upper lip just below the nose? Stimulating all three at the same time produces full body orgasms. And that there are nerves that lead directly from the bottom of a woman's feet to her vagina? Now I know why Beth loves those foot massages. And the paintbrush thing looks like something we're going to try out soon.

Pretty light fare, but if you're easing your way into the world of adult videos, this is a good way to go. You don't have to buy; they're for rent at most video stores.

PLAYBOY: THE ULTIMATE SENSUAL MASSAGE
PENTHOUSE: THE ART OF MASSAGE

If *Penthouse* won the Battle of the Dueling Tantric Love/Kama Sutra tapes, then *Playboy* gets the nod on this face-off.

Both tapes are fairly light as far as the sex is concerned, but *Playboy* gives a lot more information and is not all that much tamer than the *Penthouse* version. The *Penthouse* gals seem mostly concerned with giving a cursory rubdown, shedding their clothing, and hopping on the guys for some simulated sex, while the *Playboy* femmes actually give a good massage with voice-over instruction. I think the basic rule in a how-to tape should be that you must learn something while watching, otherwise you might as well just rent a regular erotic video. With *Playboy*, I learned.

A word about the male performers in both tapes. If all the men in regular adult videos were as good-looking as the guys in these tapes, there would be a huge response from female viewers. These guys are really handsome. Too bad they don't seem to want to make the crossover into mainstream adult erotica. Note to big-time erotica producers from women viewers: Spend some money on top-notch, newcomer male performers rather than just signing up more of the cookie-cutter, surfer-babe women and it will show up in the profit column for years to come.

One last word. I tried out my newly learned massage technique on Beth, who gave it an enthusaistic thumbs-up. "It was great," Beth said, "as long as you don't use too much of that sticky stuff." Those were very expensive Tantric Love Oils specially purchased for the occassion, Beth. Not "sticky stuff."

SELFLOVING

Good Vibrations.

This is an in-depth look at author Betty Dodson's two-day sex seminar for women on the art of masturbation. It features ten naked ladies lying around a room talking about spiritual sexual matters and being instructed by Dodson on the finer points of self love.

Be advised that the ten ladies are just regular people, ranging in age from twenty-eight to middle fifties and while some are fit and trim, some are not. The talk is serious late-sixties feelgood-speak, but everyone has a lot of laughs in the course of the course. It all builds to the final exam where everyone switches on the vibrators and goes to it. At one point the roar of the vibrators actually drowns out the sound track. All ten ladies seem to have the sought-after orgasms, which is always erotic to watch.

I picked up a few good tips on vibrator technique, especially one where a lady seems to get off by placing the vibrator *on her forehead!* I tried it on Beth and she said it didn't give her an orgasm but it did make her headache go away.

Women might find this tape instructional, but this is not a tape for lying around and watching if you want a serious evening of romance.

Sex: A Lifelong Pleasure Series
Volume 1: Enjoying Sex

Available from Good Vibrations

Beth and I really liked this series of advice tapes from Holland, featuring helpful instruction, stimulating visuals, and just enough boring parts to give you time to practice the advice. A series like this can be an easy introduction to erotica, or even be useful as therapy, if your sexual relationship with your lover could stand some improving. Consisting of scenes of Goedele Liekens and Dr. Michael Perry providing sexual guidance alternating with semi-hard-core scenes of a couple making love, these tapes can be a nice change of pace from the usual erotic fare, although they could stand improvement in some areas.

One problem lies in the hosts. Did Beth and I believe that Goedele is a sexologist and psychologist from Belgium, or that

Perry is a sexologist from Los Angeles? Sure, we went along with that. Did we care? No. I wanted to see Goedele follow some of her own advice, but Beth didn't respond to Dr. Perry. No matter, the good doctors remain totally professional throughout.

The couple on the tape is good-looking and their activity realistic. Unlike performers on most erotic videos, these two are truly "making love," and that realism is often quite arousing. We could have done without all the graphs, but these tapes do offer both effective advice and stimulating visuals. Now, if they'd only get Goedele into some sexy lingerie . . .

Chapter 4

Golden Age Films: The Classics

The Golden Age of erotic film (1977–84) produced a number of films that were long on story and high in production values. Real movies, in other words, designed to be seen in regular theaters. They also contained hefty amounts of X-rated sex. The acting is usually not star quality, but often it's as good as standard Hollywood B movies. Most people who are professionally interested in erotic videos feel these films were the best ever made, hence the term Golden Age.

Golden Age movies were shot on film stock. They had real production values, relatively high budgets, actual story lines, and shooting schedules that lasted more than a day. These movies were originally shown in theaters, until many community censors, whose job was to define a local decency standard, decided that they were just too incendiary for the average American viewer. Theater owners were threatened with legal action, and this type of movie, after a brief heyday, was abandoned by producers.

And then along came affordable videotape players, and the genie was out of the bottle.

Many of these Golden Age films are readily available through mail order if they're not carried by your video store. The classic

Devil in Miss Jones, directed by Gerard Damiano, *The Devil In Miss Jones Part II,* directed by Henri Pachard, *Roommates,* with Samantha Fox, Kelly Nichols, and Veronica Hart, and *3 A.M.,* directed by Robert McCallum, Orson Welles' cameraman for the last fifteen years of his career, are just a few of them, some of which are reviewed below.

DEBBIE DOES DALLAS

Caballero. DIRECTION: *Jim Clark.* CAST: *Bambi Woods, Merle Michaels, Robin Byrd, Christie Ford, Arcadia Lake, R. Bolla, Eric Edwards, David Morris, Herschel Savage, Jake Tegue*

This movie is a trip back in time, back to the days when bell-bottoms and afros were king. Even on white guys. What a hoot.

Debbie, one of the cheerleaders on her high school squad, has been accepted as a Dallas cheerleader, but her parents won't pony up the plane fare to Texas. She enlists the help of the rest of her squad in collecting enough money to go. The other school girls decide to really make some extra money and go to Dallas with her, to lend their support. At first the jobs are washing cars, baby-sitting, working in a library and sporting goods store. Then Debbie finds that men will pay real money just to look at her breasts. And touch them. The girls decide that this is the way to make the big cash, so they pitch in wholeheartedly.

It's really odd to watch these folks. The girls are supposed to be sixteen and some of them really look it. These are not the bronzed, implanted, shaved, perfectly buffed bodies of the nineties. These women look like real people. I guess they were the erotic stars of their time, but they look more like the amateurs of today.

I've said it before, and I'll probably say it again, these classic films are a refreshing change from the slick tapes now being made. While watching, I keep wondering who were the stars and who were just guys and gals they stopped on the street and said, "Hey! Wanna make a sex film? It'll be lots of fun!" And folks just dropped what they were doing and went along. Hell, I probably would have.

Rent it for a laugh. Check out the clothes. It might have been 1978, but it still looks a lot like the Summer of Love.

THE DEVIL IN MISS JONES

Arrow Film and Video. DIRECTOR: *Gerard Damiano.* CAST: *Georgina Spelvin, Claire Lumiere, Sue Flaken, Harry Reems, Marc Stevens, Levi Richards, Gerard Damiano*

Considered a true classic, this film has made a ton of money over the years. The problem is, it's a real downer to watch. The first of the adult sex films to deal with serious subjects like death, suicide, and rape, it loses out on our basic criteria for adult films, which is having fun and enjoying yourselves.

The plot revolves around Georgina Spelvin's character, a middle-aged spinsterish women who has lived a dull life. She kills herself, goes to Hell, and is given a second chance among the living, which she seizes with great sexual abandon. The sex is graphic, but as we said, the mood is bleak. We feel this is a rental if you really like the Golden Age tapes, or if you're interested in the history of the business, or even just interested in Georgina Spelvin. But, for a lighter evening, rent . . .

THE DEVIL IN MISS JONES II

VCA. DIRECTOR: *Henri Pachard.* CAST: *Georgina Spelvin, Jack Wrangler, R. Bolla, Ron Jeremy, Jacqueline Lorains*

This is a comedic continuation of the more serious original, and is the one to watch.

When you're in Hell, according to this movie, sex is allowed, but orgasm isn't. Georgina is brought in to make the Devil, played by Jack Wrangler, come. She does so, producing a pretty amazing flame-thrower special effect.

For this accomplishment, Georgina is allowed to go back to earth and spend eternity immersed in sex. The devil and his chief advocate keep watch on Georgina through a TV-type of machine. Not exactly the level of special effects you'll see in *Star Trek: The Next Generation*, but you have to remember this film was made about a quarter-century ago.

Georgina is transported into a succession of bodies: call girl, female soldier, Tupperware saleslady, nun, and call girl again. All of these various ladies have sex scenes.

As all of this progresses, the Devil watches and becomes more and more anguished over the loss of Georgina, until finally he abdicates his underground throne and shows up on Earth to claim his love.

There are a lot of laughs in this movie, the acting is first-rate, the costumes elaborate, the women are natural-breasted and un-shaven, and the sex is all very nicely done.

The usual problems with classic films are here—the color is a little weird, at times the story moves a tad too slowly, and it can seem dated, but those are just quibbles. This is a funny movie that you'll watch to the end.

THE DEVIL IN MISS JONES III AND IV

VCA Pictures. DIRECTOR: *Gregory Dark.* CAST: *Lois Ayres, Jack Baker, Paul Thomas, Tom Byron, Ron Jeremy, Steve Powers, Keli Richards, Erica Boyer, Tamara Longly, Marc Wallice, Purple Passion, Kevin James*

These two are considered to be lesser efforts, and we have to agree.

All of the *Miss Jones* movies after number two are very raun-chy. I could see a couple locking themselves inside an isolated cabin for a weekend and watching all five, one after another, just to prove how tough they are. You'd get a quick course in the history of modern erotic films from the Golden Age to the Modern Era, but I wouldn't recommend such a course to beginners or the physically weak.

If you want to prove you can really take it, skip these and rent number five.

DMJ5: THE INFERNO

VCA Platinum Plus. DIRECTOR: *Gregory Dark.* CAST: *Juli Ashton, Kelly O'Dell, Rowan Fairmont, Ariana, Serenity, Amanda Addams, Darcy McDaniels, Dave Hardman, Frank Towers, Arti Choke, Dave Cummings, Jeanna Fine, Nick East, Colte Steele, Hank Rose, Michael J. Cox, Nikole Lace, Marc Wallice, Joey Silvera, Mark Davis, Tom Byron, Tammi Ann, Vince Voyeur, Cal Jammer, Barbara Doll, T. T. Boy, Dallas, Sindee Coxx*

This latest version of *DMJ* is a veritable who's who of modern erotic films. This review really belongs in the hard-core section, but we've put it here because it's the latest installment in the series. Unfortunately, unless you're a real professional viewer (beginner couples, don't try this at home!) you should probably stay away from it.

This film has old people, a dwarf, fat people, pierced bodies, acres of tattoos, double penetrations, gang bangs galore, bad words, bad puns, ridiculous accents, multiple sex toys, and foot fetishism. The production values are excellent with lots of high tech effects.

The story this time around ... Miss Jones, a sexually repressed young lady, ends her life and is condemned to Hell. The Devil, played by an aging, rather tubby Rip Hymen in a non-sexual role—thank Heaven, we really didn't want to see him naked—explains why she has been condemned to the pit. Various sexual scenarios ensue, kicking off with a lady fire-eater who plays with torches and has sex with T. T. Boy while Ashton watches and allows two oldsters (Arti Choke and Dave Cummings, what's with these old guys anyway?) to fondle her.

If you really want to walk on the wild side, go ahead and rent it. But don't blame us if you get burned.

DRACULA EXOTICA

VCA. DIRECTOR: *Warren Evans.* CAST: *Vanessa Del Rio, Samantha Fox, Marlene Willoughby, Christine Deshaffer, Jamie Gillis, Eric Edwards, Randy West, Ron Jeremy*

This retelling of the classic Dracula story has some of the faults of the old timers, like an early rape scene, but the benefits far outweigh the problems.

Jamie Gillis is terrific as Dracula. The story revolves around the count as he searches for a woman who resembles a virgin he raped five hundred years before. The special effects, especially in a sex scene between Dracula and two of his undead handmaidens, are riveting. Just when everything seems to be getting too heavy, they toss in some comedy to lighten up the mood. Beth and I both liked this one, and forgave them the early rape scene.

IN LOVE

VCA. DIRECTOR: *Chuck Vincent.* CAST: *Kelly Nichols, Joanna Storm, Jerry Butler, Jack Wrangler, Michael Knight, Samantha Fox, Veronica Hart, Susan Nero*

Considered by some to be the most artistic of all erotic films, this Golden Age effort opened in regular theaters to excellent reviews. Like most tapes from this era, this suffers from color shifts in the film stock, but if you can overlook that aspect, the rather soap-opera plot, and once again the bell bottoms and sideburns that date the film, you'll find a very enjoyable tape.

Jerry Butler is a young man visiting Florida on business. He meets Kelly when he chases off two teenagers who are attempting to steal her purse. Through comic misadventure, he is thought to be the thief and is thrown into jail until Kelly sobers up and straightens out the mistake. They argue for awhile, then fall in love. And then make love.

Here's what's so different about this movie, and others of the Golden Age era. (Besides the fact that there are real sound tracks, the people can act, and all the cast and crew use their real names in the credits.) The characters make love when it is normal and appropriate to do so. In so many of the modern tapes, the characters leap into the sex on the slimmest of pretext, or none at all. Here, when in real life two individuals would naturally make love, so do the characters in the film.

Jerry and Kelly have three days of love (in the sex scene Jerry does *not* pull out when having an orgasm), and then he must fly back to his wife. The rest of the film shows us the lives of these two characters as they have their downs, and then ups.

Jerry has to sleep with his boss's wife, then he's fired. He tries various schemes related to his chief interest, the restaurant business. He wears bad leisure suits, grows his sideburns too long, and has his credit card canceled.

Kelly lives with a folk singer, joins a commune, gets tossed in the slammer for drugs, gets out and lives with a lesbian she met while in jail (no girl-girl sex scene, against my expectations), writes a novel, sells a million copies, and begins a life of luxury. She marries a movie studio exec who loves her.

Jerry opens a series of trendy restaurants called Whitlow's and makes millions of dollars.

But through it all, over a span of twenty years, they remember each other and their great love. Even though there are sex scenes as the characters meet other people, never does the sex sink to pure exhibitionist gratuity. Again, the sex is simply part of the natural progression of the character's lives. And as such, it never feels exploitative.

Finally Jerry sees Kelly's picture on the back of a book and begins to search for her. After many missed opportunities, they are reunited.

If you're a newcomer to these tapes, don't rent this film first.

Save it for after you've seen some of the modern examples so you can appreciate what might have been if the forces of censorship had never won their community-standards platform and banished sexuality from mainstream filmmaking.

THE OPENING OF MISTY BEETHOVEN

VCA. DIRECTOR: *Henry Paris.* CAST: *Constance Money, Terri Hall, Jamie Gillis, Ras Kean*

This 1976 film is often said to be the best erotic film of all time. But seeing this movie derailed my erotic film viewing for many years.

Why? Here's the story.

Years ago, Beth and I went to see this film in a regular theater. This was in that short period of the Golden Age when such a thing was possible. The lines were long and waiting to get in was an exercise in group bonding. Everyone in line knew we were going to see a sex film and any embarrassment in doing so was quickly dispelled by the circuslike atmosphere. Those were heady days, the spirit and hope of Free Love were still extant, if slightly tattered by the slowly dawning realities of the Age of Aquarius.

The doors opened and we all filed in.

I had to wait while Beth used the ladies' room, but we still got pretty good seats. So we watched the film, which is a clever erotic takeoff on the *My Fair Lady* theme. Jamie Gillis wagers that he can turn an ordinary girl into the sexiest and classiest woman of all time.

Just as we are well into the scene where Constance Money is fellating one guy while masturbating two others, Beth says, in a loud voice, "I can't find my umbrella!" "Shh," I say, trying to calm her down. She would have none of it. "I left it in the rest room, and I've got to go get it." "Okay, okay," I say, "Go get the damn thing."

Pretty soon she comes stomping back. "It's not there! Someone stole my umbrella!"

People are beginning to stare at us. Onscreen, folks are having fabulous sex, orgies are in full swing, giant private parts are swaying to and fro (they had really big screens in those days) and Beth is still bitching about her umbrella. "It was my favorite umbrella. Why would anyone steal it . . ." On and on she went.

Finally the movie was over, but Beth was still steamed. Somehow, the connection— sex = lost umbrella —had been seared into her brain. I offered to buy her a new umbrella; in fact, I offered to buy her a hundred umbrellas! But it was too late. She hated sex movies. She would never go to another in-theater sex movie. The Golden Age came and went, leaving us in the dust.

So years later, I made up for all those missed opportunities. I'm watching them all on tape, which isn't the same, but what's past is past. And now, just in case, I've bought at least a dozen of those cheap umbrellas you get on the streets. There's one in every room of the house, one in the trunk of both cars. In fact, every once in a while one of the kids asks, "Dad, why do we have so many umbrellas?"

They'll never know.

Oh, the movie? It's pretty good but I would never say it's the best erotic movie of all time.

SEX WORLD

VCA. DIRECTOR: *Vincent Spinelli.* CAST: *Leslie Bovee, Annette Haven, John Leslie, Joey Silvera*

This is a Golden Ager that was a takeoff on two early Michael Crichton Hollywood films, *Westworld* and *Futureworld.*

It always astonishes me to see the production values on these classic films after having watched a bunch of modern tapes. The film opens up with twenty or so couples boarding a bus after an airplane flight. The bus has a huge Sex World sign posted on the side. Then, while the couples are introduced via flashbacks, we see the bus driving along the highway in traffic. There are lots of location shots of the bus zooming along. As I watched the sequence I kept thinking that just the expense of the shots of the bus alone would be higher than the entire budgets of most modern shoots.

Anyway, all of the various individuals and couples have some sort of sex problem, and the long weekend visit to Sexworld offers them answers.

Each couple checks into their room, then has an interview with a counselor, who sets up their experience. The impotent man, his frustrated wife, the lonely woman, the hot-shot racist, the elegant lesbian, etc., are cured of their difficulties in interesting ways.

Two of the usual Golden Ager problems are evident: bell-bottom pants and afro hairdos, but these are easily overlooked as most of the people take off their clothes pretty rapidly. The bodies are all real, the hair unshorn, the performers attractive.

This is considered one of the best Golden Age erotic films ever made, and we agree. We were disturbed by the racist guy (played by John Leslie) who draws a black woman as his partner—the dialogue is chilling to our modern sensibilities—but he learns a damn good lesson, so I guess we'll let it slide.

Rent it. You'll watch it from beginning to end and not be sorry you did.

SMOKERS

VCA. WRITTEN, PRODUCED, AND DIRECTED BY Veronica Rocket. CAST: *Sharon Mitchell, John Leslie, Joanna Storm, David Christopher, Diana Sloan, Eric Edwards, Ron Jeremy, Troye Lane*

Here's an example of one of the Golden Agers that you should probably stay away from. It's known as a cult film, and as such has its devotees. We're afraid we're not among them.

John Leslie is an actor in this one and it's obvious why he was such a great talent. He's good-looking and he can really act. The perennial Ron Jeremy is here as well, and he's thin, got all his hair, and is quite funny in his role.

The story has to do with a female revolutionary known as Madame Suque, who just wants to blow up the Establishment. She puts a bomb in a vibrator so she can smuggle it somewhere or other, and of course the infernal device falls into the wrong hands. The rest of the film follows Madame and her henchmen as they try and locate the missing vibrator.

The problem is, there's a fair amount of staged violence and nonconsensual sex. None of it is very realistic, but still, I don't like it and neither does Beth. In the course of the film they indulge in spanking, slapping, bondage and discipline, a fling with fruit and vegetables, and lots of whacking people over the head with fake bottles.

I believe the purpose was to entertain those with bondage-and-discipline interests, and one scene of a woman tied up over a twisting vibrator is undeniably powerful, strange, and erotic. If your interests lie in these directions, go ahead and rent it. Like most Golden Agers, the production values are good and the actors are all competent or better, we just didn't like the violent angle the film took.

Chapter 5

For Couples Only:
Andrew Blake

*B*efore you start this chapter, be sure you've read the section on Andrew Blake in Part One, Chapter 11. And remember: Blake is a sensual, atmospheric director—the quintessential couple's filmmaker. If you're looking for slamming raw sex, look elsewhere.

We've seen all of Blake's films, and we review and recommend every one of them. They're all much alike, which is fine with us. None has ever really disappointed.

Because of the vignette structure of Blake's films, the reviews will mostly list and describe the separate scenes.

DESIRE

VCA. CAST: *Zara Whites, Savannah, Kelly Jackson, Amber Lynn, Jeanna Fine, Viviana, Nina Alexander, Zorena, Randy West, Jennifer Kingsley, Brad Gerig, Capri Danell, Peter North, Marc Wallice, Bridgette Monroe, Tera Heart, Blake West, Jon Dough, Ashley Lauren, Marc Francis, Casey Williams*

If you're interested in watching beautiful folks making slow sensuous love, here's your evening's rental.

The lovely Zara Whites, one of Blake's favorite actresses, appears in most of these scenes, though often as an onlooker rather than a participant.

The action kicks off in the art gallery while Zara watches Jon Dough and Savannah make love on a couch. Long, slow, and lovely to look at. Not much real heat, but this is an Andrew Blake movie. The scenery is just as important as the sex.

A bunch of people then have sex on a staircase: some watch, some participate, some masturbate. Peter North shows his legendary ability to produce massive quantities of semen.

Zara and Marc Wallice make love by one of those fabulous pools. Very nice.

There follow five or six more scenes, most of which are much the same as in all Andrew Blake films. All are beautiful, all are low-key, nobody does anything out-of-line, everybody looks absolutely terrific while they do it. There is one long scene where a painter rolls paint on a small herd of beautiful women then sticks them on big sheets of canvas and makes interesting pictures. This is an engrossing scene, but one feels sorry for the artist, who gets a couple of free feels but no real sex from the starlets.

This tape is a high-class effort from the always high-class Blake.

Hidden Obsessions

Ultimate. CAST: *Janine, Heather Hart, Steve Drake, Randy West, Julia Ann, Melanie Moore, Francesca, P. J. Sparxx, Kym Wilde, Peter North, Marc Wallice, Skye Blue, Paula Price, Deidre Holland, Jon Dough*

This is one of our favorite Andrew Blake films. The women have never looked more beautiful, and the sex is steamier than usual.

A rich man has a request. His wife, whom we never see, has unusual needs. She desires exotic, erotic fantasies and the rich man hires Janine to provide them. She's a writer, so she has this ability. (All us writers are like that.)

Janine is one of the leading stars in the business and when

you see this movie you'll know why. She's very elegant and very beautiful, and Blake is just the man to showcase these traits. As the writer, she comes up with a dozen or so scenarios that would move even the most jaded wife: straight hetero, girl-girl, orgy, and kinky.

The action is filmed in the usual Hollywood upper-class mansions with terrific views and fabulous furniture. The production values are on par with anything Blake has ever done, the camerawork and lighting are perfect.

Then there's the scene with the double-headed ice-cube dildo.

I've seen this done since in other videos, but never as well as here. Janine and Julia Ann are alone outdoors in some sort of crow's nest overlooking what I assume is Hollywood. They have a dildo made of ice that must be damn near two feet long. They use this dildo in various inventive ways.

During this scene I noticed Beth watching with a peculiar intensity. By the time they are done, the dildo is a mere icicle of its former self.

That's the highlight, and there are no lowlights at all.

This is a must-rent.

HOUSE OF DREAMS

Caballero. CAST: *Zara Whites, Jeanna Fine, Raven, Veronica Dol, Saber, Ashlyn Gere, Randy Spears, Rocco Sefreddi*

An early Blake and one of the least plot-driven tapes. But, like most Blake productions, it's got classy-looking performers in upscale surroundings doing what they do best. All of the action takes place in and around one of the fabulous houses that Blake uses for his locations. This one is modern: severe, ascetic, minimal. It goes very nicely with the lovely Zara Whites.

We open on Zara all by herself, lying on a white bed, idly masturbating. A few words about Zara: She's absolutely stunning. Blake seems to favor her above all other actresses, and it shows in his camera work. He never twists her into convoluted positions, never puts her into an undignified situation, always photographs her in the most flattering light. They are a team, and a damn fine one. You're not going to get a lot of heat from Zara, but that's not why we look at Andrew Blake films. Here we're looking for atmosphere, nuance, and beauty. Key words in a couple's film.

You supply the heat.

Back to the story, what there is of it. Zara has a double-exposure, out-of-body experience. She arises from the bed and watches herself. A strange machine appears in the room. She is suddenly bathed in an odd red-blue light while she and several other women have sex with a man.

The machine disappears.

A seashell appears. She picks up the seashell and she is suddenly on a beach, where she sees two nude women sleeping, wrapped in a fishnet, and one of them is herself. A fellow comes along, frees the women, and has sex with one while Zara watches and employs the seashell.

Dream sequence time. Rocco and Raven ravish Zara, beautifully, of course. Then she has solo sex with a four-foot-long lighted neon bulb. No, no, she doesn't use it *that* way, this is an Andrew Blake film. Just kind of rubs herself with it. Another woman with another light bulb joins her. This is a classy scene, the tension deriving not from sexual heat, but from the fact that these two ladies are fooling around with *glass light bulbs!*

The glass motif is carried through the last scene where a small mirror breaks, and Randy West appears and has sex with Zara. The scene is filmed reflected off the pieces of shattered glass.

Zara wakes up.

Amazing. What won't Andrew Blake try next?

This is not a "hot" tape. This is a great background tape. Put it on, turn off all the other lights in the room, watch awhile, fool around, dip back into the tape, let the lovely colors play across your bodies . . .

You get the idea.

LES FEMMES EROTIQUES

Ultimate. CAST: *Julia Ann, Dahlia Grey, Raven, P. J. Sparxx, Sunset Thomas, Deborah Wells, Kelly O'Dell, Christine Tyler, Marc Wallice, Randy West, Peter North, Aaron Colt*

As we've noted above, if inane dialogue, cheesy sets and costumes, unattractive performers, and improbable sexual setups are holding you back from fully enjoying erotic videos, this may be the film to change things for you. Essentially plotless, the movie is a series of vignettes, loosely strung together, but it is light-years beyond the average compilation tape typically showcasing the glories of the male orgasm. The film features a professional score, costumes both elegant and fetishistic, wonderful indoor and outdoor settings, and all of it rivaling any multi-million dollar mainstream Hollywood production. Not to mention the great-looking, supermodel-quality men and women in the cast.

Most of the actresses have avoided the surgeon's knife, and those who didn't went to excellent doctors, with nary a visible scar. The men are muscular and well-endowed. The sexual liaisons are natural and romantic, and for the most part, the men wear condoms. We have a minor quibble with the persistence in even these highest-quality erotic videos of the man coming on the woman, but only two are facials. Without a word of dialogue save moans of (seemingly) genuine ecstasy, each scene flows easily into the next, and each one seems sexier than the last.

The film opens with "Fantasy Girls," starring Raven, Dahlia Grey, and Julia Ann. The trio, dressed in tight leather, rubber, and vinyl, are trying several virtual-reality devices, and the plot premise is that all that follow are VR fantasies. Our first fantasy is "High-Tech Love" with P. J. Sparxx, Raven, and Mark Wallice. P. J. Sparxx's body is so exquisite I can even forgive her those idiotic pedal-pushers she's wearing. Set in as fine a mansion I've seen outside *Architectural Digest*, P. J. and Mark make love on a leather ottoman. Raven joins them.

Among the other episodes is "Glass Bedroom," starring Deborah Wells in a short solo scene. As she sensually strokes her body, the color fades to sepia. The art direction and production design throughout the film are top quality.

"Staircase Lovers" stars Julia Ann, Sunset Thomas, and Aaron Colt. I loved the women's earrings in this one. It's this attention to detail that can often make the difference. "Ballet Shoes," in black and white, stars Dahlia Grey and Julia Ann and the ultimate pair of spike heels. "Blindfold" stars Julia Ann and Randy West. Julia's dress is amazingly beautiful and Randy's suit alone would eat up the budget of the average erotic video. Randy keeps his suit on and makes love, condomed, to Julia through his open fly; somehow it's one of his most erotic performances.

"Malibu Morning" stars Dahlia Grey and P. J. Sparxx in a rough/tender scene that has them literally ripping the clothes off each other.

"Fornicon" ends the tape with a bizarre tale that melds the look and feel of Fellini and Helmut Newton and stars Julia Ann and Raven.

Aside from a couple of facials, which I must confess I don't *entirely* dislike, we can find little fault with this film. It is beautiful to look at and listen to, and each narrative could stand with the best scene of any erotica tape. *Les Femmes Erotiques* is a guaranteed-good-time couple's film.

NIGHT TRIPS

Cabellero. CAST: *Tori Wells, Porsche Lynn, Randy Spears, Victoria Paris, Peter North, Ray Victory, Jamie Summers, Tanja De Vries, Marc De Brun*

Tori Wells has a problem: She can't sleep. She's tormented by dreams of a sexual nature, keeping her constantly aroused. The tape opens up with Tori alone, doing what these ladies are always doing when they're alone. She decides she has to go to the doctor.

Her kindly doctor, Randy Spears, has called in an associate, a sexual psychologist, who has brought along her "mind-scan imager" to help solve the problem. They stick a couple of leads to Tori's thighs and tell her to go to sleep. Then they watch her pleasure herself as she dreams about another couple having sex, which they watch on the monitor of the mind-scan imager. This couple uses an ice cube in ways a lot more interesting than Mickey Rourke did in *9½ Weeks*.

Tori goes into an even deeper sleep, where she fools around with a black feather and a gold dildo.

One of the leads falls off Tori's leg, and when the psychosexualtherapist puts it back on, this triggers a girl-girl fantasy in Tori's dream.

The doctor and therapist decide that the therapy isn't working. They show her some slides and tell her she needs to become aware of and not suppress her feelings about sex. Good advice. Then she watches another woman have sex at a swimming pool with a handsome black guy. This is a pretty sexy scene, though the black guy is not as adept as some of the old hands. His inability is somehow touching.

Then two people in masks come in and begin to have sex. Tori joins them. Who could these two people be?

It's the two doctors! What a surprise! Tori goes home and uses the telephone—no, no, not for that, she makes a phone call. Soon, a man enters and they have sex. She says, "I have a few fantasies I'd like to try out on you." Finally we see the man's face. It's the doctor!

She says, "Thanks, for everything."

He says, "Anytime, love."

End.

Hey, I've already said you don't watch an Andrew Blake film if you want scintillating dialogue. Andrew's smart enough to know (many aren't) that we don't watch these movies for what the characters say, but for what they do.

NIGHT TRIPS II

Caballero. CAST: *Randy Spears, Cheri Taylor, Racquel Darrian, Erica Boyer, Cameo, Tami Monroe, Lauren Hall, Bridgette Monroe, Nina Alexander, Briana Bal, Randy West, Eric Price, Jon Dough, Derrick Lane, Paula Price*

I think *Night Trips II* is a better movie than its predecessor. Mostly I think that because the doctor, once again played by Randy Spears, has a nurse, Cheri Taylor, who looks a lot like Angie Dickinson. I like Angie Dickinson.

Paula Price takes the Tori Wells role of *Night Trips*. Her problem? She just can't get enough sex. We open with the standard solo scene in a bedroom. Paula decides she has to see a doctor, so she goes to the mind-scan foundation. There, Dr. Randy Spears says she needs to learn sexual control, so he hooks her up to his machine. She "dreams" she's having solo sex in a bathtub. (Shot in sepia. Very nice.) She gets out of the tub and has sex on the bed with a man.

The nurse and the doctor discuss the case and decide she needs to be probed by the "Dream Activator." Paula then has sex with two other girls by a pool.

The doc says to the nurse, "This woman is extraordinary! There's no diminishing of her sex drive!" By now, the doctor and nurse are so turned on by all this activity that they rip off their clothes and make love on the floor. Very nice scene. The nurse is a mature woman with a great body and still looks a lot like Angie Dickinson, even with her clothes off. Not that I've ever seen Angie Dickinson with her clothes off.

Meanwhile, Paula is having more fantasies and has entered "level six," where she finds Randy West, another guy, and four women. Randy West has on a great leather jacket which he takes off very reluctantly and only after several pairings. Much of this action takes place on the staircase, showing once again that these filmmakers love to shoot sex on steps. Maybe it makes the filming easier.

Suddenly, for no apparent reason one of the girls has sprouted vampire teeth! Then Randy has vampire teeth as well! Then Paula says, "Oh! The vampires, the vampires are coming!" Neither Beth nor I had the slightest idea where this plot twist came from or was going to.

Then we're back in the doctor's office. He writes out a prescription for a "sexual suppressant." She's to start weekly therapy.

In the last scene, Paula is back at home. Alone. The pills obviously have failed.

Sure, the story doesn't make much sense, and those vampires really came out of left field, but most viewers probably aren't going to get this far in the movie anyway. Not because it isn't good, but because they'll be distracted by each other by this time. But that's what it's all about anyway, isn't it?

It's a good rental or purchase. Trust us.

SECRETS

Caballero. CAST: *Ashlyn Gere, Zara Whites, Samantha Strong, Rocco Sefreddi, Jeanna Fine, Danielle Rogers, Saber, Sunny McKay, Fallon, Nona Alexandre, Randy West, Valerie Stone, Krystina King, Nicole Wild, Kristen, John Dunn, Peter North, Brian Williams*

The story here concerns Ashlyn Gere, one of my personal favorite performers, who plays a Beverly Hills madam with a stable full of beautiful girls and a roster of moneyed gents. Ashlyn spends most of her time riding around in a limo dressed in very little while she relates her story. She remembers her favorite client, Nick (Rocco Sefreddi), and we flash back to Nick riding in the limo. He gets a phone call, suddenly orders the car to stop, and leaps out.

Puzzled, Ashlyn remembers how Nick was the best. Another flashback to her and Nick, making love in a designer reclining chair. While they're at it, someone is taking pictures of them through a large plate-glass window.

She drives around Beverly Hills making solo love with a diamond tennis bracelet as she recalls other clients and girls.

Danielle (Zara Whites, Blake's favorite actress) is looking

through a telescope on the balcony of a home high in the hills. She is watching Randy West have sex with four beautiful women. Probably just another day for Randy in Beverly Hills. While she watches, Rocco comes up behind her and pleasures her.

(One question you may have—at least this viewer does—as you watch an Andrew Blake film, is where does he find all these fabulously beautiful women and how does he convince them this is the career choice to make?)

Next she tells us about another girl, Ashley, who has a Navy officer (Peter North) as a client. North is working on a Top Secret document when Ashley comes in. They have some champagne, she coaxes him out of his nice white uniform, and they make love. After, she slips a pill into his champagne and while he's sleeping she steals the Top Secret documents!

Ashlyn, the madam, tells us about the exquisite German, Petra, who likes to dress up like a man and have sex with one of the girls.

Then we have Thomas, the head of a film studio, who wants only virgins. He has one in the garden of his fabulous home.

Ashlyn tells us, while using a split of Moët Chandon in place of the tennis bracelet, about the two sheiks who hire her girls to have each other while they throw (obviously fake) hundred-dollar bills on them. The sheiks don't do anything in this scene except toss around their money.

Ashlyn gives Nick (Rocco, in case you've forgotten) the Top Secret document, and then she and another girl make love to him beside a lovely pool overlooking L.A.

One last scene, where the madam tells us about Conrad, who is also into kinky sex. Conrad is an old man who, thank God, only watches as two of the girls make love while employing a riding crop to tickle each other. (One of the women is Jeanna Fine, who is notable here for not yet having had her breasts worked on.)

Then we're back in the limo, which drives by a newsstand. We see a headline that says CASINO MILLIONAIRE CAUGHT WITH

CALL GIRL. Then she knows it was Rocco's wife who photographed them and told the newspapers.

The End.

While the story ends rather quickly, it doesn't really matter as we've had our usual Andrew Blake experience: beautiful performers, fabulous locations, interesting and varied sex with little dialogue to get in the way of the erotica. As usual, a solid rental.

SENSUAL EXPOSURE

Ultimate. CAST: *Kelly O'Dell, Debi Diamond, Marc Wallice, Mark Davis, Raven, Deidre Holland, Kristi Lynn, Melanie Moore, Peter North, Heather Hart, Devon Shire, Mimi Milagi, P. J. Sparxx*

It's the age-old story: A young girl must learn the secret rites of sex so she will be ready for the man she desires. She goes to one of those fabulous L.A. mansions where she is to begin her education. A series of scenes then unfolds as she wanders around, sometime joining in, sometimes working solo. There's no real story. Who cares. We're in Andrew Blake–land.

One image has, as Mark Twain used to say, joined my permanencies. Raven and Debi Diamond have a wordless scene in which one is literally tethered to the front end of a carriage and the other, half-dressed in riding outfit complete with leather crop, urges her mare/woman on. No sex, just this incredible visual image. Wow.

There's more, much more, but it is that one scene that has me asking, not for the first time, and not for the last: How does Andrew Blake get these beautiful women to do these things?

Chapter 6

Not For Tough Guys Only:
Hard Core

AMERICAN GARTER

VCA. DIRECTORS: *Henri Pachard and Gloria Leonard.* CAST: *Seka, Tyffany Million, Steve Drake, Randy West, Ona Zee, Mike Horner, Tim Lake, Joe Verducci, Sierra, Nicole London, Melanie Moore, Tony Tedeschi, Joey Silvera, Heather Hart*

This is one of our all-time favorites. Although a modern film, you could put this film in the Golden Age section and no one would ever notice. It's set in 1961 and the costumes and sets are perfectly faithful to that era. It's a tribute to all those films about bright sassy women and the bumbling males who think they're the ones who are running the show. I half expected Katharine Hepburn and Spencer Tracy to walk on-screen and start bickering.

The American Garter company is readying itself for the Big Spring Show. The conservative designs of senior lingerie designer Seka are about to go head-to-head with those of eccentric, avant-garde boy-wonder Tony Tedeschi.

Before the show begins there's lots of interoffice sex. Ona Zee in the accounting department shows her staff of two what the top lady is capable of. Several of the girls stop off in the ladies room for a bit of fun and find plumber Joe Verducci working away. He gets a nice surprise. Then madman Tony Tedeschi gives two of his models a taste of his wackiness as one of them swings through the air on a girdle tester, and Joey Silvera as the harried tailor/fitter gets punished for pricking one of the models with a pin. Backstage at the big show, everyone gets in on the action.

Meanwhile, the girls are parading down the runway in a multitude of girdles, bras, and exotic underwear.

The story is told in voice-over, and the funny Brooklynese commentary is one of the key elements that puts this film over and above virtually all others.

The production values are high throughout. I kept checking wristwatches and other details to catch the filmmakers in some time-continuity mistakes, but I didn't see a one. The film itself is shot in colors that recall a movie made thirty-some years ago, and the costumes and hairdos of the women complete the effect. Even though most of the actors and actresses in this effort are the usual cast of characters, you hardly recognize them.

Which brings us to Seka, one of the great older erotic actresses who makes her comeback here and shows she still has what it takes to keep up with the younger generation. I think she should rest on her laurels with this one, and not make the mistake of staying in the sport well past time for her to go. Great job, Seka. Go gently into that good night.

Beth enjoyed this one as well, but she's just enough younger than I am to have missed the, well, not joys, but athleticism it took to work your way into one of those rubberized girdles. It's this element that gives *American Garter* its funny, kicker ending, where the girls win big and the men all retire from the field happy, but certainly not victorious.

This is a must-rent for a funny, sexy evening.

BAD HABITS

VCA. DIRECTOR: *John Leslie.* CAST: *Deidre Holland, Tyffany Mynx, Randy Spears, Mark Davis, Sasha Strange, Angel Ash, Deborah Wells, Tom Byron, T. T. Boy, Jon Dough, Ted Craig, Dyanna Lauren*

This film's first sex scene could only come from John Leslie: Deidre Holland watches in a warehouse basement as four men stand in the shadows masturbating as Dyanna Lauren puts on a latex outfit, then they each orgasm in turn on her bottom. Beth found the scene very arousing, although she didn't like the harsh jazzy score and I thought the spotlight in the background was a little blinding. I know, I know, picky, picky, picky.

A large potted plant conceals much of the action in the next scene between Tom Byron and Deidre Holland. Deidre plays a writer who recounts her numerous sexual activities to psychiatrist Randy Spears, but soon determines he's a quack. He blackmails Mark Davis into seducing Deidre, but they fall in love and turn the tables on him. A scene between Randy and his receptionist, Tyffany Mynx, contains some very erotic wordplay. Speaking of wordplay, Randy tosses around some Shakespeare; I've noticed that a Spears role often has literary subtext. I don't know if it's Randy's doing or not, but as a writer, I appreciate these little touches.

This isn't one of Leslie's best efforts, though it does have good acting and story, but that also means it doesn't reflect some of his weirder tastes. And I always enjoy seeing the sex life of a writer so accurately portrayed.

BLONDE JUSTICE II

Vivid Film. DIRECTOR: *Paul Thomas.* CAST: *Janine, Summer Knight, Alex Jordan, Tyffany Mynx, Jessica Fox, Lacey Rose, Tony Tedeschi, Nick Rage, Tim Lake, Terry Thomas*

This is a Janine star vehicle, and not much else, so if you're not a big fan of hers skip it unless the really good stuff is out of the store. Sometimes on a late Saturday night when you've got a hankering for some erotica, you just have to settle for second tier. Unless, like I say, you're a Janine fan. There's a lot of her in this movie.

Skip *Blonde Justice* and go straight to the sequel. That way you won't have to watch both of them to find out who the bad guy is.

Janine works in a strip joint and is being hassled with threatening letters by someone, a crazed fan, co-worker, or local madman. Policewoman Alex Jordan takes on the personal assignment of protecting her. Most of the sex is girl-girl (Janine only performs girl-girl scenes) and much of it takes place onstage in front of an appreciative audience. If you like to watch the ladies dance, this is one for you.

Real mystery fans will see the end coming a mile away, though the identity of the killer is a surprise. Well, a mild surprise.

Hang on for the credits at the end. There's a wonderful shot of Janine strapped to some sort of giant wheel. The wheel of justice, I guess, grinding slowly. Whatever it is, it's an arresting image.

BLUE MOVIE

Wicked Pictures. DIRECTOR: *Michael Zen.* CAST: *Jenna Jameson, Steven St. Croix, Jeanna Fine, Tony Tedeschi, Tera Heart, T. T. Boy, Lana Sands, Dallas, Rebecca Lord, Alex Sanders, Jordan St. James, Jackie Beat, Roadblock*

This is another one of the more-than-slightly wacky movies that Beth and I both like. It has a Blue Ball, about the size of a regulation soccer ball, that talks and makes love to women; a transvestite movie director; and a female tabloid publisher who looks and acts like the legendary, now-deceased Divine of John Waters fame.

The movie opens with a very sexy scene between transvestite Steven St. Croix and his psychiatrist. She straddles him and slowly pulls up her dress. "I want you to talk to my pussy," she says.

"Hello," he responds, staring it right in the, er, eye.

Her pronunciation of "heterosexual" with a French accent is both funny and sexy.

St. Croix's agreeing to dress in Carmen Miranda drag for the duration of the movie certainly shows his sense of humor as well as his self-confidence as one of the industry's top performers.

The next scene has Jenna Jameson masturbating with the talking Blue Ball, which was both funny, strange, and sexy all at the same time. The plot connection to the talking ball is tenuous at best, but who cares?

Jameson stars as a cub reporter investigating the movie set of cross-dressing erotic director St. Croix. The movie-in-a-movie gimmick allows for scenes unrelated to the story, including a very sexy one with Jameson and T. T. Boy. While on the set, Jameson learns such insider info as the function of a fluffer. If you don't know what a fluffer is, rent the movie and learn, or just read the glossary herein.

Jackie Beat's nonsexual drag role as the female tabloid publisher is very funny, St. Croix has a real love story with his tough female bodyguard, and all the pieces fall into place in the end. *Blue Movie* has humor, steamy sex, and the distinctive Michael Zen polish. If you like your movies slightly offbeat, this is a must-rent.

BONNIE AND CLYDE

Vivid Video. DIRECTOR: *Paul Thomas.* CAST: *Ashlyn Gere, Randy West, Racquel Darrian, Derrick Lane, Nikki Dial, Francesca Le, Alex Jordan, Mickey Ray, Nick E., Jonathan Morgan, Tom Chapman*

All the stars in this movie speak with Texas accents. It's a little unnerving when you first hear Ashlyn and Randy, who play the crooks on the run, twanging away at each other.

The idea of the movie is obvious. The producers spent some

big money on this one: costumes, period cars, and sets. The action cuts back and forth between Bonnie and Clyde, the rest of the gang, and the bored Racquel and her hick sweetheart in their rural country town. Eventually Bonnie and Clyde hook up with Racquel and her boyfriend, who no longer find life quite so dull.

Ashlyn doesn't look as fine as she usually does. It's the costumes; they make her look a bit frumpy. Randy West, on the other hand, has never looked so good. This is Randy at his prime, big and beefy, before he stopped dying his hair, obviously having a great time with his role as the consummate gangster. But it's Racquel who outshines them all. She looks terrific in her loose country frocks, which are always falling off.

Bonnie and Clyde rob banks, drive getaway roadsters, and join up with the rest of the gang who are busy having outdoor sex at the hideout. The FBI is hot on their trail.

None of the sex is really blazing, but I didn't mind. The story is engrossing enough to keep your interest, the acting is good enough to not intrude, and you're always aware that Racquel's dress is due to come off in the near future.

This turned out to be a two-parter and I found myself being mildly interested in seeing the second part. That's rare with these films.

BONNIE AND CLYDE: PART TWO

Often the part two of one of these tapes is just leftovers from part one re-mixed and glued together. Not so with this one. In fact, I'd say you should see part one if you're going to make any sense out of part two. Not that the story line is particularly complex, but just to figure out who the characters are and why they're doing what they're doing.

The story continues in the same vein as part one. The gang back at the shack is captured pretty much without a whimper. I guess they were tuckered out from all that outdoor sex.

Racquel and her big boyfriend really hit it off with Bonnie and Clyde. Meanwhile the two G-men who have been haunting the countryside begin to close in on the two outlaws. Jonathan Morgan, playing one of the G-men, Billy Bob, continues to prove, in my humble opinion, that he's the best actor in the adult business.

The bandits decide it's time to flee the countryside, so they decide to rob another bank. But first, they trade partners and have an interlude with Racquel and the boyfriend. Then it's off to rob the bank.

In the woods, the two G-men wait. Up drives who we think are Bonnie and Clyde, then we see that it's Raquel and her man. They explain to the G-men that they stopped to help two strangers in a broken down car, and that they ended up trading cars and clothes. A little hard for this viewer to believe, but the G-men fall for it and Bonnie and Clyde are on the run again.

The sex herein is all excellent. Again, at least for this reviewer, Racquel steals the show, but all the performers are good-looking and enthusiastic.

BORDERLINE

Vivid Film. DIRECTOR: *Paul Thomas.* CAST: *Tyffany Million, Steven St. Croix, Celeste, and a whole town full of Mexicans*

I have to say this tape was, well, borderline for me, but it was saved from oblivion by my wife who gave it the nod.

The film opens with a straightforward sex scene between Daniel and Brandy (Steven St. Croix and Tyffany Million, respectively). I found the scene particularly workmanlike, and as I don't much care for Ms. Million's rather feral look in this particular tape, I FF'd through it to get to the story.

Daniel is cheating on his wife. He says he is going on a business trip, packs his bag, hops into his Mercedes convertible, and drives off. We cut to Julie, played by Celeste, who is sending her fat but rich husband off to work for the day. His concern is what she'll be cooking for dinner that night.

Julie meets Daniel, and off they go for a trip to Mexico. So much for her husband's dinner.

In Mexico the car breaks down and they end up in a strange little town. They are staying in a large but rather broken-down hotel. While they have sex they are watched by an inquisitive maid.

The main theme here is that Julie is a fun-loving gal who optimistically sees the glass as half full. Daniel is grumpy and keeps yelling at everyone—the mechanic who is working on his car and the staff at the hotel. He sees the glass as half empty, and whoever drank the top half is in serious trouble. He's a pain.

Julie has an encounter with the maid at the hotel (on the steps, which is a frequent venue for sex in these tapes, for some odd reason). The maid has a number of unusual silver studs placed in various areas of her body. This is a pretty good scene, but cranky Daniel comes in and breaks it up. Too bad.

Later they meet a charismatic Mexican at a strange restaurant where a TV screen shows films of people having sex while the patrons eat chips and salsa. Daniel continues being a pill, and Julie is attracted to the Mexican.

After several strange sexual interludes between the local inhabitants in what is becoming an increasingly odd town, the action takes us to the final scene, set at a big festival at the home of the charismatic Mexican. There, naked ladies play the parts of bulls to lucky matadors, the partygoers become increasingly sexual, and soon most everyone is rutting in the dust. This scene is something that Luis Buñuel would have been proud of, and while it was not particularly *hot*, it was so surreal that you had to believe that the director intended it to be so. High praise for this genre of film. The townspeople are obviously played by locals.

After the party scene, the car gets fixed and our mismatched couple go back to their former lives. Julie finally tells Daniel that he is a pill (hooray), throws her glass of champagne in her fat husband's face (atta way, girl), and goes back to the strange village and her handsome, enigmatic, Mexican.

In retrospect, I have to say that I liked this tape more than I thought I did when I began this review. Technically, it looked like a second-rate movie, which means it was a first-rate erotic video. The actors actually acted, and if the sex wasn't incandescent, it was sometimes unusual and the performers were uniformly attractive. Celeste, the actress who plays Julie, has implants the size of water balloons, which I don't find particularly attractive, but that's the norm in the industry and she's certainly beautiful in every other way.

Don't put it at the top of your list but it's definitely worth a rent.

CASANOVA

Sin City Video. DIRECTOR: *F. J. Lincoln.* CAST: *Rocco Sefreddi, Tabatha Cash, Flame, Skye Blue, Tracy West, Tina Tyler, Randy West, Bridgette Monroe*

This is a tape we recommend for one stand-out scene. For the most part, the tape is decently made with high production values and competent acting, but the story is slightly confused.

It's a bit unclear, but Rocco seems to be the reincarnation of Casanova, or maybe he never really died. Anyway, he now has a sister, Tabatha Cash, and they live in upscale surroundings and continue the Casanova traditions.

Rocco has his way with Tina Tyler in an armchair and Tabatha has Bridgitte Monroe in the bathtub and then Randy West by a fireplace. All of it is fine, but it's Rocco and Flame on the, yes, you guessed it, staircase, that earns this tape a recommendation.

This scene shows you just how hard these performers work. Flame is a natural red-head who starts out the scene in Victorian period dress and impeccable makeup and ends it shorn of any manmade artifice. Rocco turns her every which way, for a while upside down, and at the end they are both sopping wet from one end to the other, inside and out.

Rent it if you don't feel like wading through an entire tape and just want a quick jump-start of your own. FF until you see Flame begin to descend the staircase. An amazing scene.

CHAMELEONS (NOT THE SEQUEL)

VCA. DIRECTOR: *John Leslie.* CAST: *Deidre Holland, Ashlyn Gere, Rocco Sefreddi, Jon Dough, P. J. Sparxx, Fawn Miller, Tim Lake, Mickey Ray, Tracy Wynn, Brandy Alexander, Sunset Thomas, Zach Thomas, Candace Hart, Nick E., Leanna Foxxx, Woody Long*

I remember seeing a trailer for *Chameleons* on another erotic tape and thinking that it looked like it would be a good movie even without the sex. And, for the most part it is. I've certainly seen mainstream Hollywood do a lot worse.

John Leslie is one of the finer directors pioneering the new wave of erotic videos—35mm films with a coherent, well-written plot, an accomplished, good-looking cast, and sex that is both arousing and furthers the storyline. The movie is subtitled *Not the Sequel* to distance it from another Leslie film called *Chameleon* starring Tori Wells.

Chameleons opens with Ashlyn and Jon Dough and entourage arriving by limo to a party at a warehouse. On the steps, Ashlyn berates an intoxicated member of her group and has one of the women have sex with him. The scene is confusing, but it does let Ashlyn show off her acting; she's one of the most accomplished in the business.

The action moves to the party/orgy. All too often in these tapes, parties consist of the entire cast gathered in a room having sex while synth music plays on the sound track. This is a party that actually looks and sounds like one: plenty of guests, loud music (a zesty salsa number), dim lighting, and people dancing and talking as well as having sex. Deidre Holland follows Ashlyn into the bathroom, and in a transformation scene lifted from

Adrian Lyne's *Jacob's Ladder*, assumes the form of Rocco Se-freddi. Their sex scene is *very* stimulating.

Later at their home, Rocco tells Deidre that each time she imitates him, it saps his strength, killing him. She says she can't stop. They have a tender sex scene.

Ashlyn visits Deidre and wants to learn the chameleon technique. There's a definite sexual tension, a will they/won't they? anticipation to their scene together that you don't usually find. And when Ashlyn reaches into Deidre's pants and finds Rocco's penis, it's actually shocking. Leslie has managed to infuse his scenes with suspense. Ashlyn wears a strap-on dildo and makes love with Deidre. It's a bizarre scene, but very erotic.

A later scene illustrates those characteristics that make this film stand out from the rest. Ashlyn initiates sex with Rocco, but he pushes her away when she reveals a hidden agenda. When's the last time you saw someone turn down sex in an erotic tape? In films of this caliber, story takes precedence over sex.

Rocco fades away, his power gone.

Jon Dough arrives, looking for Ashlyn, who seduces him after assuming the form of Deidre. She has become a chameleon. Ashlyn picks up two stranded motorists on the way home and, after changing into Jon, has a threesome. This is the only conventional scene in the movie.

Later, we learn what has actually happened: Rocco has been Ashlyn since she tried to seduce him. His power returned, he is reunited with Deidre. Don't worry, it's not this confusing when you actually watch.

This was one of the first films we saw that transcended the mainstream erotica genre. It has a good plot, fine acting, and a unique directorial voice. It's as good as many a mainstream film. And, taking the sex into account, it might even be better.

CLIMAX 2000

A Virtual Production. DIRECTOR: *Michael Zen.* CAST: *Tyffany Million, Kaitlyn Ashley, Mike Horner, Leena, Buck Adams, Vixxxen, Tony Tedeschi, Nikki Sinn, Jon Dough, T. T. Boy, Nick East*

A computer hacker uses virtual reality to invade the world of erotic movie-making in this well-scripted, well-performed, sexy film.

Tyffany Million starts things off with a solo scene, then has a performance with Tony Tedeschi that goes a little past the point of comfort for Tyffany. Beth really doesn't like it when it's patently obvious that the woman would like to call a halt to the sex, so you can FF towards the end of this scene if that bothers you as well.

Buck Adams has a nice time with love doll Vixxxen, whose pierced clit makes a few interesting appearances. Tyffany simulating fellatio with a virtual Nick East is an oddly arousing scene. All the performers are exciting.

Michael Zen, the hot new director, is certainly good at balancing sex and story, but occasionally a sex scene is marred by overuse of technical effects intended to imitate virtual reality—and the film does have a downer ending. Still, a touch of science fiction, a behind-the-scenes look at erotica, and a dash of *All About Eve*, make *Climax 2000* a very sexy glimpse into the future.

A CLOCKWORK ORGY

Pleasure Productions. DIRECTOR: *Nic Cramer.* CAST: *Kaitlyn Ashley, Isis Nile, Jon Dough, Alex Sanders, Rebecca Lord, Nikole Lace, Jonathan Morgan, Olivia, Shelby Stevens, Dick Nasty, Kyle Stone, Vince Voyeur, Jay Ashley*

This is a takeoff on Stanley Kubrick's *A Clockwork Orange*. I'm not sure how you would take to it if you haven't seen the movie it is based on. Kaitlyn Ashley, as Alexandra, takes Malcolm McDowell's role as Alex in the original. The writer has used the

Anthony Burgess lingo and added some of his own variations while leaving most of Burgess's inventions.

Alexandra is the leader of her all-girl band of "droogs" who are mostly interested in "the old ultrasex." They roam the sometimes seedy, sometimes chic environs of their vision of the future, harassing males and forcing them to have sex with the gang.

The sets are terrific, from the junkyard to the exotic milk bar. They used a number of locations for this shoot and spent some real money. It shows.

Unfortunately, Kaitlyn Ashley is not quite up to the dramatic level her role requires. The language is tricky and when she acts next to Jonathan Morgan, who is terrific as the Warden, she is completely blown away. I've said it before, but anyone who thinks erotic stars can't act, check out Morgan in this tape.

The film follows the original movie fairly closely plotwise, and adds a lot of explicit sex. There's all the usual variations, boy-girl, girl-girl, etc., and while I didn't find the sex particularly blazing, it was always entertaining.

(A word here about fingernails. Those ladies always have these really long nails. I cringe when I see a girl-girl scene with those long nails. And how about that square-cut look that the ladies are sporting these days? Beth tells me it's called a "French cut.")

The element that made this film for me was the humor injected into the action. It crops up just when things seem to be getting too serious. When Alexandra is taken to jail she stands before the jailer and is told to empty her pockets. This is funny to begin with because she's in a skintight white jumpsuit that doesn't have a pocket anywhere. She proceeds to produce and slam down on the table a set of handcuffs, a vibrator, a strap-on dildo, and a plastic inflated penis that is about four feet long and a foot in diameter.

In the end, this movie did what all good takeoffs should do, it made me want to see the original. If you haven't seen *A Clockwork Orange*, you can rent it at most video stores. Look for it in the sci-fi or horror sections. Then you can check this one out, and you'll understand what's really going on. If you don't want to rent the original, I think you'll still think this one is pretty cool.

COMPANION

Vivid Film. DIRECTOR: *Paul Thomas.* CAST: *Ashlyn Gere, Asia Carrera, Tera Heart, Sandi Beach, Randy West, Steve Drake, Nick East, Dallas, Guy DeSilva, Paul Thomas, Evan Daniels*

This is one of the mystery plots, an often-used convention in erotic films. Dallas is the wife of emotionally disturbed Randy West. She is killed very early on, after a sex scene with the pool guy. (I used to think that the pool guy was just an erotic movie convention—the bored California woman needs to seduce someone convenient—until I recently read that Robert Duvall was divorcing his wife because of her ongoing liaison with *their* pool guy.) Randy West witnesses this encounter and dashes off, acting very weird indeed.

Two detectives trying to find out what happened to Mr. West's wife are then introduced. (One of the detectives is played by the director, Paul Thomas, who had his own career as a male star in mainstream and erotic films. See the section on directors.) Both detectives are competent actors, as are most of the other performers.

There is a relatively complicated plot dealing with this mystery, but it doesn't really interfere with the sex, which is usually very good. Ashlyn Gere is always fine to watch, as she can really deliver a heated sex scene, and Asia Carrera as West's private secretary is particularly beautiful. As of this writing, Carrera has not fallen victim to the breast augmentation mania that has engulfed the industry, and her natural body and lovely face are well presented by director Thomas.

There is some violence in this film, but it is presented in the context of the dramatic story line, so I had no problem in that regard. It was still 500 percent less violent than most regular R-rated films.

The photography level is consistently high, and the use of unusual effects (black-and-white flashbacks, slo-mo, etc.) contributed to the excellent overall effect, making this a solid rental.

CYNTHIA AND THE POCKET ROCKET

Cal Vista Films. DIRECTOR: *Jim Enright.* CAST: *Jessica James, Anna Malle, Kristy Waay, Jordan Lee, Tony Tedeschi, Peter North, T. T. Boy, Steven St. Croix, George Kaplan*

All too often, erotic video parodies of mainstream Hollywood films never progress farther than a (occasionally) clever mocking title. *Forrest Hump, Edward Penishands, Bonfire of the Panties.* And the subjects of caricature are usually well-known box office hits. So when a relatively unknown movie like *The Hudsucker Proxy* is spoofed—Beth and I are among the thirty-seven people who saw this mainstream film—and its title is *not* the lame and obvious *Cocksucker Pussy*, you stand up and pay attention. *Cynthia . . .* is the story of Cynthia Thudsucker (played by Jessica James), a small-town girl who comes to the big city and invents the vibrator. While the film suffers from poor acting, the superior quality of the sex and the sheer obscurity of the source material make this one highly watchable.

Steven St. Croix stars in the first scene as the owner of a toy company making love to two ladies. He dies in their arms, but not before he offers them jobs in his company. T. T. Boy is a mailroom clerk who befriends Cynthia. He has a steamy scene with an actress who coerces him into sex. T. T. is a terrible actor, true, but I sometimes enjoy the halting way he speaks his lines. He's trying hard, and his superlative swordsmanship makes up for any thespian shortcomings. Tony Tedeschi has several good scenes. The video ends with T. T. and Jessica finally getting together.

The lovemaking in every scene is exciting, and the oral sex is particularly erotic. The authentic 1950s props, hairstyles, and costumes are a nice touch. The acting is generally amateurish, but the fact that they're attempting such an unusual spoof—and it's very sexy besides—makes this one worth viewing.

THE DINNER PARTY

Ultimate Pictures. DIRECTOR: *Cameron Grant.* CAST: *Crystal Gold, Celeste, Kaylan Nicole, Debi Diamond, Misty Rain, Daisy, Asia Carrera, Yvonne, Kylie Ireland, Juli Ashton, Tammi Parks, Vanessa Chase, Norma Jean, Vince Voyeur, Nick East, Sean Michaels, Marc Wallice, Gerry Pike, Mark Davis, Randy West*

The director, Cameron Grant, is an Andrew Blake kinda guy, and that's what you get, mostly, in this high-gloss film.

Steve Drake is the host of the dinner party, held in a mansion overlooking some faraway city, which I assume to be L.A. Everyone is dressed in gowns and tuxedos. Over dinner, which no one seems to be eating, Steve encourages the guests to recount their innermost sexual fantasies. As each one does so, we get to see them enacted. First off, one of the ladies recounts an outdoor fantasy involving two guys who ride up on horses. The next is a kitchen scene where two of the ladies get covered with flour and butter and lots of milk and other stuff and roll around on the chopping block. This looked pretty uncomfortable to me, but mostly I envied them their kitchen, which was a lot nicer than mine.

There's a cool arty scene shot on a blue bed; a construction worker bit with Asia Carrera; a scene shot through a fountain; one in a strange boiler room where two women tell a guy what to do; and an unusual scene where Sean Michaels is in a plate-glass cage and masturbates while watching a woman strip and writhe. Very interesting.

But the winner is a three-way girl scene that takes place in a gynecologist's office. This turned out to be an award winner and it deserves it. Debi Diamond, Misty Rain, and Celeste go at it with Ms. Diamond going nuts all over the office, upside down, on the table, backwards, forwards and every other which way. I'll never look at a string of pearls in quite the same light.

The actors appear a bit wooden when not performing sexually, but in this case, who cares? In the end everyone leaves the dinner table, and goes to the living room for some expensive brandy and a first class orgy.

Bon Appetit.

THE DIRTY WESTERN II

Cal Vista Film. DIRECTOR: *Adele Robbins.* CAST: *Lisa Ann, Brittany O'Connell, Valeria, Fallon, Brooke Waters, Morgan Phoenix, Ian Daniels, J. P. Anthony, Adam Vaughan, Rick O'Shea, Tony Cortez, Andrew Wade, Bobby Rodeo, Titus Moody*

Evidently there is a *Dirty Western I*, which I've never seen, but I don't think I've missed anything starting with the sequel. This is not *Lonesome Dove*.

The producers spent some money here. It's as far from the one-bed-in-the-hotel-room-with-two-people-having-sex aesthetic that you're going to get. These folks wear costumes, which they keep on for much of the time. They ride on a stagecoach, which was probably not that cheap to rent—including the horses—and lounge around in what appears to be a well-kept ghost town that they must have hired out for a couple of days.

There seems to be something of a plot, but I never really understood what was going on because the sound was not very good. The story centers around a bunch of bad guys, who never do anything really bad except play the guitar, which they do pretty badly. A team of dance hall girls seem to be employed in keeping the bad guys busy so they don't do anything bad except play the guitar and keep their hats and boots on when they make love.

I was leery of this film because the tape box talked about the gang members, which worried me that there was going to be some sort of stupid violence angle. As noted earlier, thankfully this element is not normally part of these tapes these days, as proved true here. This is a good-humored production.

The cast is all good-looking and while the screen sex is never truly steamy, it's a fun movie if you're in the mood for a "ride 'em cowgirl" kind of entertainment. There is also a comic actor who does nothing except sit around with a silly little grin on his face. His name, according to the credits, is Mr. Gilbert.

(As already mentioned, the sound is bad in this film. This is one of the real weak links in these videos. I recommend always putting a tape on and checking the sound as soon as you get home so you can take it back and get another tape if it is hopeless.)

DOG WALKER

John Leslie Productions. DIRECTOR: *John Leslie.* CAST: *Christina Angel, Kristi Lynn, Isis Nile, Joey Silvera, Jon Dough, Steven St. Croix*

John Leslie is a talented director who started out in the business as a performer. *Dog Walker* is highly recommended, but this doesn't necessarily mean you should rent Leslie's other tapes. Like a lot of these directors, he does a number of different types of films that are not nearly as classy as this particular one.

Steven St. Croix is the thief, Tito, who after a diamond heist under the employ of a mobster, decides that he hasn't been paid enough. The mobster kicks him out and decides to take everything he has away from him: his house, his wife, his criminal career.

That's it. Seem a little thin? Well, yes, but then there isn't much story to bog down Mr. Leslie's interesting noir vision. There are a lot of unexplainable, surreal scenes here, which are all to the good as they lend a certain amount of interest to the proceedings. You find yourself saying, What the hell does that mean? which translates to viewer involvement.

The makers spent a lot of money on this film. Leslie produces some very slick and classy scenes with lots of atmosphere.

The sex? Adequate, with a few standouts, poor as well as good. The opener where Tito's wife is ravaged by two mob guys is one of the poorest in the film. The wife is not coerced in this endeavor, in fact she is all in favor of it. First the two guys beat up Tito (leaving not a mark on him), then he has to watch. Jon Dough does the actual sex, while his African-American partner sort of stands to the side and tries to keep his equipment erect. Without much luck.

To balance this rather lame effort, there is a terrific scene in the middle of the film where Steve has sex with Isis Nile in a small room that has a glass wall, behind which Christina Angel does a solo number while everyone watches each other. Christina Angel may not have quite the most beautiful face in adult films, but she has a superb body. This one scene is worth the price of the rental. Very, very nice.

John Leslie casts himself in a small part in the film and proves that as a Dennis Hopper look-and-act-alike he is unparalleled.

All of the performers are attractive, and there is even a scene with a woman who is as flat-chested as a twelve-year-old boy, proving that you don't have to have balloon breasts to be sexy. Something we all know, but the makers of these films usually don't seem to understand.

This film has won most of the major awards that the adult film industry presents, and I feel it deserves them. If you can excuse some of the sex scenes as being rather tepid, you'll find this an excellent choice.

A note about the violence in this film. While much physical mayhem is implied, very little of it is either believable or even on-screen. While it pretends to be a tough-guy movie, you get more violence in a Saturday morning cartoon, by far.

ELEMENTS OF DESIRE

Ultimate Video. DIRECTOR: *Cameron Grant.* CAST: *Julia Ann, Maeva, Daisy, Draghixa, Aaron Colt, Celeste, Woody Long, Mark Davis, Tyffany Mynx, Misty Rain, Asia, Paul Price, Deidre Holland, P. J. Sparxx, Victoria Andrews*

It's easy to get this tape mixed up with all the other tapes that use the word *desire* in their titles.

This one has a picture of a naked lady with a snake wrapped around her on the box cover. This may turn you on, or turn you off, but the snake doesn't make an appearance on the actual tape.

Julia Ann, staying up late because she isn't getting sex from her husband, or maybe just not enough sex, stumbles on a strange TV channel that makes her want to have sex and to watch the people on TV having sex. I've been looking for that channel since I was a teenager.

Too bad I never found it.

Everyone is very good-looking and the sex is just fine. We recommend this one not because of any story, but in the spirit of Andrew Blake: great-looking people doing interesting things, high production values, nice photography. Very stimulating.

'Nuff said.

EROTIKA

Western Visuals Gold. DIRECTOR: *Robert McCallum.* CAST: *Samantha Strong, Rebecca Bardoux, Nikki Sin, Vince Voyeur, T. T. Boy, Cindi Storm, Rick O'Shea, Porsche Lynn, E. Z. Ryder*

Robert McCallum is sometimes referred to as a wannabe Andrew Blake and those softer aspects do crop up in his work, but it is his artistic touches that people are talking about when they apply this comparison.

This is the story of a country girl who rejects her life and sets out for the big city. She lives in a cottage with her raggedy father who is a drunk, driven to the bottle by the unfaithful behavior of his now-departed wife. These early scenes are shown in black-and-white flashbacks that have the interesting feel of a fifties stag movie. The father is E. Z. Ryder, whom you often see listed as a nonsexual performer in erotic tapes. He must be a famous guy in this world, but I have no idea who he is, or why he keeps cropping up. Suffice it to say, he makes such a perfect scum-ridden abusive old man that I would recommend fast-forwarding through the whole first part, with a quick stop at Samantha under the waterfall with Vince Voyeur (whom Beth finds charming), and then back to the FF button until you get Samantha in the car headed out of town with T. T. Boy and Rebecca Bardoux. Definitely click on the play button with Boy and Bardoux, who come to a screeching stop in the middle of the desert for some scorching sex.

The rest of the tape is the story of a fabulously beautiful woman's rise to the top. There are some great location shots as Sam travels through Europe, falls in love, and becomes wise to the ways of the world.

This is a solid rental, with attractive actors, good direction, and good performances. But don't forget, fast-forward through the early part. You'll be happy you did.

EXSTACY

Western Visuals. DIRECTOR: *Robert McCallum.* CAST: *Tyffany Million, Sarah Jane Hamilton, Frank Towers, Steve Drake, Tom Byron, Mike Horner*

The big selling point of this movie is that it's filmed in both San Francisco and New Orleans. In a genre that takes place mostly in bedrooms, it's hard to see how this is a major marketing tool. Aside from a few outdoor shots of San Francisco, and a nonsexual scene on Bourbon Street at Mardi Gras, location plays no part in the story. No matter. This movie shines for one principal reason: Sarah Jane Hamilton.

Beth and I have always enjoyed her work, and we can't quite figure out why. It's not her looks. Though she is actually pretty, her body is very well rounded and her skin is rather pale for our taste (well, she *is* English). Beth decided it's her attitude. Sarah enjoys screwing her co-stars, and it's our luck that a camera happened to be filming at that time. She also never wants the sex to stop and urges her co-stars on even after they orgasm. What a trooper. All three of her scenes are exciting, with Steve Drake, Mike Horner, and Tom Byron. Unfortunately, she doesn't have a squirting orgasm in this film. (See *Immortal Desire* and glossary.)

The story revolves around a sex club where Tyffany Million slums as a call girl while her husband works late. Mike Horner is his co-worker who knows her secret. Mike has a very funny physical comedy scene that turns sexual. Tyffany's ruse is discovered, of course, but this only solidifies her husband's love for her. During this scene, Tyffany's breasts are lactating, a trick she performs which I find to be a total turnoff. Rent this one if you're a Sarah Jane Hamilton fan, as she doesn't get many starring roles.

FACE DANCE I AND II

Evil Angel Video. DIRECTOR: *John Stagliano.* CAST: *Rocco Sefreddi, Tyffany Million, Joey Silvera, Brittany O'Connell, Francesca Le, Cody O'Conner, Christy Ann, Sierra, Tyffany Mynx, Sheila Stone, Angel Ash, Kiss, Rebecca Bardoux, Tina Tyler, Steve Drake, Tony Tedeschi, Kris Newz, Tom Byron, Woody Long, Rick Smears, Roscoe Bowltree, John Stagliano*

Two of the great adult videos, winners of Adam Film World's Best Movie of the Year for 1993. Both contain scenes that neither Beth nor I liked, but the power of these two tapes kept us watching from beginning to end. We don't recommend watching them back-to-back, but one per consecutive weekend might be the way to go.

John Stagliano, the infamous Buttman (see *Buttman Goes to Rio III* and *IV*), proves here that he's far more than a one-trick pony, even while working his usual shtick into this movie as well.

Face Dance I opens with a gang bang sequence, even though the gang of guys is pretty small (three). My dislike of these group scenes is a personal preference, and I particularly dislike them when they hold a hint of menace, which this one does, even though it is shot in an interesting blue light with cascades of water and the woman doesn't seem to be coerced. After the scene ends we learn that it is a scene-within-a-scene, an erotic movie being shot. The director quits, or dies (I can't remember which), and Tyffany Million decides to take over.

The star of the movie, the indefatigable Rocco Sefreddi, is en route from Europe. Shanghaied by an extremely busty blonde along the way, he ends up at a surprise party being thrown by his old buddy, Buttman. There are a herd of guys and gals who, along with Rocco, strip down and get it on. This is a good group scene, with an interesting aside by one of the fellows who tells us that he is just a regular guy who wrote a fan letter to Stagliano, who in turn invited the guy to appear in one of his videos. It's little touches like this that keep me watching these movies.

Eventually Rocco gets to the movie production and thus begins the real plot of the story. Rocco's problem is that if the producers learn that he is in reality an adult film actor, it will jeopardize his position on the mainstream set. It's all sort of complicated and there are lots of scenes that seem totally improvised, but somehow it works. At one point Rocco gives an impassioned speech about the state of adult erotica in Europe that is both heartfelt and interesting, and in another scene he has a foursome that is hotter than any I have ever witnessed in an adult video.

We wish John Stagliano would make more movies like this, and spend a little less time on his Buttman series.

GANGLAND BANGERS

VCA Pictures-Capitol Film. DIRECTOR: *Joe D'Amato.* CAST: *Juli Ashton, Steven St. Croix, J. R. Carrington, Dallas, Jean Teal, Mark Davis, Roxanne, Tony Montana, Sofia Ferrari, Sean Michaels, Guy, Vince Voyeur, Pier Louis, Claudio Bergamin, Tiziana Mervar*

Set in Chicago in the 1930s, this tape chronicles the rise and fall of one Rocky Partano, played by Steven St. Croix. Rocky is a young man who has come four thousand miles from Italy to make his fortune. Starting as a dishwasher in a restaurant, Rocky heroically saves the life of a mob boss's moll and wins a spot on the boss's staff.

Frankie, the boss, hires Rocky to be his girlfriend's guardian angel—a mistake if ever there was one. But Rocky eschews carnal pleasures for the moment to set up a big liquor import deal for the boss. Frankie doesn't appreciate Rocky's go-get-'em attitude and so Rocky quits to start his own mob. Frankie tries to hit Rocky, who survives and in turn has Frankie hit. Rocky then takes over Frankie's mob, and of course, his girlfriend.

Eventually, success spoils Rocky and he abandons even his best friend in his quest for respect and fortune. The best friend takes up with Rocky's girlfriend and the circle is complete.

Another hit is put out on Rocky, this time successfully, and Rocky crashes to earth in slow-mo as the bad guys put the finish on his meteoric career.

And during all of this many people have sex with each other in varied and inventive ways.

The fun here is picking out the anachronisms. Rocky uses a lot of slang that wasn't around in 1930, he drinks straight vodka from a bottle of Stolichnya, one of the hoods sports an earring, and the head bad guy wears a ponytail. At one point Rocky is shot in the arm, with blood all over his shirt. An hour later he is in bed with his girlfriend and there's not a scratch on him. Fast healer, that Rocky. And then there's the chief moll. Do you think it's possible that in the thirties she would have the Grateful Dead dancing bear tattooed on her groin? Cute, but I don't think so.

This movie is fun. They spent a bundle on clothes and cars and sets. The acting varies wildly, but what the hell, I didn't really expect Steven St. Croix to sound like a goombah. Production values are high, the dialogue sound, as usual, is poor, but the music (by Peter Mountain) is far better than the usual synthesizer mush.

Pour yourself some bathtub gin, fire up a smoke, slap in this tape, grab your moll or gangster, and enjoy yourself.

IMMORTAL DESIRE

Vivid Visuals. DIRECTOR: *Phillip Christian.* CAST: *Sarah Jane Hamilton, Dyanna Lauren, Gerry Pike, Tony Tedeschi, Debi Diamond, Lady Paree, Angela Baron, Brad Armstrong, Colt Steele, Serenity, Alex Sanders, Sasha Savage, Tony Martino*

This is an excellent tape for newcomers. The film has very high production values and lots of good-looking people. The shooting and editing are high-tech and professional. What it lacks, for us, is heat. Even though there is a fire dance.

The story line, such as it is, has Sarah Jane Hamilton as some sort of sorcerer who reincarnates herself through the ages into different bodies. We start off with a WWI sequence (a setting I've never seen explored before in adult films), drift through a voodoo scene, then through a bunch of other stuff. I wasn't paying much attention because I kept wishing for more *heat.* But I did keep watching because it was very well made and I, being an Adult Film Professional Viewer, knew that Sarah Jane Hamilton is known as a squirter (see glossary), and I wanted to see her do her thing.

Eventually, she does.

The problem here, if it is a problem, is that after you watch these tapes for a while, you get a bit jaded. You want more. I know I'm playing right into the hands of the censorship folks, but it's true. The Pat Robertsons of the world would probably say that after watching for a few more years Beth and I will turn into raving sex maniacs who go on a cross-country spree raping and pillaging our way through the heartland of America. I guess Beth will have to ask for time off from work for this rampage. No, it's not going to happen, we'd never find anyone to watch the kids while we were gone.

So if you're an experienced viewer, I'd say give it a pass. But if you're early into your watching, or even a first timer, or want to see one of the famed squirters, this would be a great tape.

JOHN WAYNE BOBBITT UNCUT

Leisure Pictures. DIRECTOR: *Ron Jeremy.* CAST: *John Wayne Bobbitt, Nikki Randall, Jane Chen, Tyffany Lords, Veronica Brazil, Ron Jeremy, Letha Weapons, Jordan St. Clair, Crystal Gold, Jasmine Aloha*

This is one to stay away from. I only include it because the curiosity/novelty angle might lead some people to rent it. Don't bother. John's penis is not very large and the only evidence of his famous injury is a raised-flesh kind of scar that rings the base. (John has recently had a penis-enlarging operation. In an interview John said he was very pleased with the results. "It's as big as a beer can," he said. You *could* see it in his latest video, *Frankenpenis*, but you don't want to, believe me.)

The video quality is poor, and John sounds just as dumb as you supposed. He has a difficult time maintaining an erection, and most of his co-stars appear to loathe him. There's more heat in a fresh load of laundry than there is between John and his partners.

For the inside story of this shoot, see the section on male performers earlier in the book.

JUNGLE HEAT

Adam & Eve. DIRECTOR: *Joe D'Amato.* CAST: *Rocco Sefreddi, Rosa Caracciola, Nikita Gross, Swetta Schulter*

I thought I was going to laugh all the way through this one, but this remake of the Tarzan myth gets very high marks for technical expertise, beautiful performers, sets, locations, and story. In other words, it actually looks like a real movie. In fact, it looks like an old-time *Tarzan* movie, only without Johnny Weismuller and plus a lot of sex.

Rocco Sefreddi, as mentioned earlier, is certainly one of the legends in the industry—for his looks, physical endowment, and capabilities. He can also act, which puts him at the top of the male-performer heap.

Most of these location movies look as if they're filmed in Southern California or in warehouses, which most of them are. I was skeptical in the beginning, but when Tarzan and Jane walk across a beach into a flock of startled flamingos, I had to admit that either they really were in Africa or they had spent a lot of money on flamingo extras.

The story is simple and follows the Ape Man myth, at least in spirit. Jane discovers Rocco in his loincloth, which is soon lifted; they have an interlude in the jungle; Jane is rescued and brings Tarzan back to the hunting lodge and puts him into a tuxedo and takes him to dinner. In the course of two days Rocco pleasures every woman in the party and one of the lodge maids.

All of the performers are fine looking, and as it was a foreign production, the women are not the usual actresses we see in most American films. This is a nice change. The sex is not what I would classify as volcanic, but it's all well performed and easy to watch and reasonably stimulating.

I really don't have a single complaint about this movie, except that whenever Rocco gives out his Call of the Ape Man they use the Johnny Weismuller original, which startled me into memories of childhood Saturday mornings spent in front of the TV set. Definitely an unsettling experience while watching Tarzan have his way with Jane in the crotch of a tree.

In the end, sadly or perhaps triumphantly, Tarzan elects to abandon civilization and go back to the jungle to resume his life of solitude with the animals. I think he was just plain tired out from having sex with all those women.

It's dubbed from some other language, but that doesn't matter. Sex is the universal language. Rent it.

LATEX

VCA. DIRECTOR: *Michael Ninn.* CAST: *Sunset Thomas, Jon Dough, Juli Ashton, Tyffany Million, Jeanna Fine, Emerald Estrada, Lacey Rose, Barbara Doll, Jordan Lee, Tasha Blades*

This is perhaps the greatest erotic film of the modern era, absolutely deserving of the Best Adult Movie of the Year award it won in 1995. If you like science-fiction movies, and are willing to deal with some kink in your sex, this is a must-see tape.

Now for the disclaimer...

I like strange films, and this one sure fits the bill. So, be advised that viewer discretion is suggested, and if you're in over your head here just hit the eject button and pop in a Femme film.

Like most Ninn films, I couldn't begin to tell you what it's about. Like most Ninn films, I didn't really care.

Latex is a science-fiction saga, and Ninn deftly blends a high-concept, dense plot, with blistering sex and fetishism. Jon Dough plays the main character, Malcolm Stevens, a psychiatric patient with psychic abilities. His mental gift lets those he touches experience their deepest sexual secrets. Jon Dough's performance, nonsexual for much of the film, is astounding for an erotic video. The man can really act. His primary sexual turn in the film comes at the end, when he is covered, head to toe, in skin-tight latex. Sunset Thomas has never looked so good, poured into her latex chauffeur's uniform. Their scene together is one of the most amazing of any erotic video I've viewed. Dough, wearing a prosthesis (credited in the end credits as the

Megasplash), orgasms cups—no, quarts, no, *gallons*—of semen all over Thomas. If you enjoy a cum shot, this is the be-all and end-all of the genre.

Jeanna Fine gives a fine performance in a ménage à trois and a tearful acting scene. All the sex is steamy and features tight latex wear and fetishistic dress in abundance. Ninn's films were tailor-made for the slow motion button on your remote. Ninn has embraced computer technology for his films and creates very believable futuristic worlds. Computer-generated sets, camera shots, and morphing effects invent a future that pays homage to *Metropolis* and *1984*. If you can't comprehend the plot of this film, just be amazed at the production value and the eroticism presented. You won't be disappointed.

Rent it or buy it. Pass it along. Amaze your friends. And about this latex thing, I never really understood that particular fetish.

Until now.

THE MASSEUSE: PART ONE

Vivid Video. DIRECTOR: *Paul Thomas.* CAST: *Randy Spears, Hyapatia Lee, Viper, Danielle Rogers, Porsche Lynn*

I've read that this movie won several Adult Video News awards and I'm sure it deserved them. The next time someone says erotic actors can't act, have them rent this tape.

This is basically a two-person story. There are a few other actors in the film, but they have only small parts.

Randy Spears plays a shy, socially retarded librarian who is a twenty-eight-year-old virgin. He goes to a massage parlor for sex, and meets Hyapatia Lee. The sex, along with the story, unfolds very slowly in this film.

Spears plays an extremely unusual character, the likes of which I've never seen in an adult film. He is *so* shy, and *so* inept, that you figure he's just got to be some sort of perverted murderer. Paul Thomas, the director, does nothing to disabuse us of this notion. Spears plays out all the trappings and actions of your basic stalker. He calls Hyapatia at home, he tells her he loves her, he follows her home, he badgers her at work, and all the time she treats him in a sympathetic and realistic manner. She tells him that he has problems, that she can't work them out for him, and even though she has sex with him he must help himself and not rely on her.

Hyapatia's acting is almost as strong as Spears. She is utterly believable in her role, even when Spears follows her home and finds her with a husband and baby.

The sex between them occurs in very measured steps. From the early scenes in the massage parlor to the last lovemaking on his bed, Hyapatia gently teaches Spears how to overcome his shyness and make love to a woman. In a way, all of this sounds like a basic screwy erotic video plot, but in Thomas' hands it really isn't. The evenness of the whole approach makes the sexual build-up much more interesting than what is usually depicted, and only adds to the eroticism.

In the end, you find all your pessimistic projections to be unfounded. Marketers often say that various tapes are really different. They usually aren't. This one is.

At one point, when Hyapatia first comes to Spears' apartment, she looks at his books and asks if he's a reader. She picks up a book, James Agee's *Let Us Now Praise Famous Men*, and asks him what it's about. Ostensibly it's about southern sharecroppers, he says, but it's also about life, and different ways of seeing things. "One of the great poetic pieces of literature, by one of its greatest practitioners," he says.

She opens the book and reads, "Everything that is, is holy." After their sex scene, he gives her the book.

Like I said, this one's different.

THE MASSEUSE II

Vivid. DIRECTOR: *Paul Thomas.* CAST: *Ashlyn Gere, Asia Carrera, Leena, Christina West, Steven St. Croix, Randy West, Tony Tedeschi, Carl Radford, Steve Drake*

This is a sequel that fails to live up to its predecessor. For the most part, it is a very sexy film, with Asia Carrera and Ashlyn Gere turning in stellar sexual performances, but these are overshadowed by the misogynistic nature of the story. Ashlyn plays a massage parlor girl who's obsessed with her status in life: Is she merely a prostitute? Asia plays her more grounded friend.

Asia has several blistering scenes with Steven St. Croix. Ashlyn's role, however, puts her in several distasteful scenes. When her boyfriend Steve Drake discovers her occupation, he has very rough sex with her. Randy West verbally abuses his girlfriend in a threesome. Ashlyn buys a gun and caresses herself with it (in a scene Beth found very offensive), and the movie ends when she kills herself! Though this film is a showcase for Ashlyn's acting talents, a story such as this is not what one wants in an erotic film. Stick with the first movie.

MINA IS MAKIN' IT

Vivid Video. DIRECTOR: *Toni English* CAST: *Mina, Kaitlyn Ashley, Debi Diamond, Tricia Yen, Isis Nile, Marc Wallice, Sean Michaels, Ed Powers, Jim South, Steve Austin, Wayne Wright*

If you've ever wondered about breaking into the erotic movie industry and just how it operates but didn't know who or what to ask, here's a video that answers every question from hiring to coming, and throws in some great sex to boot.

Mina Is Makin' It begins with a young man—Wayne Wright, in his introductory role—answering a dare to try out for a role in an erotic video. We sit in with Wayne and Mina, playing an aspiring actress, as they are separately interviewed by veteran producer Jim South, who explains the hiring procedure, salaries, medical precautions, etc., to them. We found this section of the video very interesting. The video then turns from informational to sexual as both Wayne and Mina quickly find work in the exciting world of erotica. Unfortunately, Wayne stars first with Debi Diamond, who's gotten so emaciated Beth refused to watch her. The sex itself is very passionate and acrobatic, but she does need some meat on her bones. The behind-the-scenes scenes are obviously scripted, but Marc Wallice has a good ménage à trois scene and Sean Michaels is a pleasure to watch as always. The combination of interesting backstage information and sex make this how-to video a have-to.

JUSTINE

Cal Vista Films. DIRECTOR: *Paul Thomas.* CAST: *Roxanne Blaze, Tianna, Lacey Rose, Dyanna Lauren, Mike Horner, Nick East, Brad Armstrong, Alex Sanders*

Justine is one of the most awarded films in adult video history, garnering Best Movie of the Year by AVN in 1993 and Best of the Year by the X-Rated Critics Organization—and deservedly so. It tells the story of a father and son, Mike Horner and Nick East, who unknowingly are involved with the same woman. It's classic movie-of-the-week fodder, yet here it is treated in a much more authentic manner than network television ever dares. In addition to providing a glimpse into the impulses that drive such a taboo, the chance encounters and missed connections that must occur during this plot are realistic and believable.

Horner plays a widower reluctant to resume dating. An encounter with Tianna ends when Horner remains unaroused. One sees impotence in erotic videos, but it's usually unintentional; here it's essential to the story (and the scene is still sexy besides).

Roxanne Blaze is new to the adult business, but she's a welcome addition. Both naturally beautiful *and* a good actress, she plays the sexually adventurous girlfriend of Nick East. She meets Horner in a sex shop where she's researching a story for a magazine. Their flirtations pack some real heat, and she convincingly talks dirty during sex as well. The moment when she discovers the true identity of her new lover is award-quality acting. The orgy scene is excellent, though I did hear the director call out one instruction. That brief moment aside, this film features some of the most plausible relationships, best acting, and sexiest romance of any film on the shelves.

NYLON

Vivid Film. DIRECTOR: *Nick Orleans.* CAST: *Celeste, Rocco Sefreddi, Tammi Ann, Laura Palmer, Nancy Vee, Misty Rain, Steven St. Croix, Bobby Vitale, Veronica Hart*

This is a very stylish film.

Steven St. Croix has a problem. He is obsessed with nylon. This, he informs us, has gone beyond fetishism. He tells us the story from the vantage point of a very minimalist, very elegant restaurant, where the decor is all done in tones of red. He sits at a table and spins his tale.

He is a photographer. His obsession with photographing and fooling around with nylon-clad women costs him his girlfriend, Celeste. When he finds a perfect nylon model, he spends all his money on her, but she won't let him sleep with her.

He tells us where it all began, in college, 1966. Three coeds in miniskirts demonstrate how pantyhose took the place of stockings and garters. This is unlike any college class I ever had; more's the pity.

His obsession costs him everything: his job, his apartment, his girlfriend, his friends. He goes to a psychiatrist, the lovely Veronica Hart. Nothing helps.

Celeste takes up with Rocco, who gives her some friendly advice on fetishism. She should indulge her boyfriend, he advises. She asks what makes him an expert. He says he watches a lot of television, and he is a writer. I wanted to leap out of my chair and shout, "I'm a writer! I'm a writer, too!"

Rocco really has a very small part in this movie, even though you can't tell from the box cover.

Anyway, while Steven is telling the camera his story, a strange woman dressed all in black sits near him on a stool in the restaurant, crossing and uncrossing her nylon-clad legs.

He finally makes a play for this mysterious woman, and she takes him home. He takes a bath and dresses up in a tuxedo and is then presented with a string of nyloned women in beautiful costumes. The crowning moment is when the woman in black comes out, now dressed all in white nylon. She pulls off her dark wig and we see it's Celeste! His old girlfriend! She's learned to not only accept his obsession, but to aid and abet it. They make love.

This all has a very cool, very hip look about it. The women, their costumes and clothing, the sets, are all done in vibrant colors that blend beautifully with the nylon motif. Everything in this film is a pleasure to watch.

LA PARFUM DE MATHILDE

Vivid Film. CAST: *Draghixa, Julia Chanel, Christophe Clark, Maeva, Elodie, Simona Valli, Elisabeth Stone, Eric Weiss, Richard Langin, David Perry, Thomas Smith, Manon, Kathy.*

If you are interested in European erotica but want to avoid the almost endemic bad skin and teeth of most of the performers, *La Parfum de Mathilde* features a great-looking cast, exotic French locations, *great* sex, and, unfortunately, one of the worst dubbing jobs since radioactive monsters destroyed Tokyo. Language interpretation aside, if your video store carries Eurotica, rent this tape. There are two ways to watch this film and ensure an enjoyable evening: turn the sound off, put on some soft romantic music, and let the sexual imagery arouse you, or watch it with sound on for a side-splitting comedy. French erotica stars say some very odd things during sex, if the translations are correct.

This story of the young bride in an arranged marriage and her discovery of her new husband's sexual appetites features super-sexy sex from the entire cast. Don't worry about the dwarf who appears in almost every scene, he has a nonsexual role. The part of the maid is played by one of the most attractive black performers we've ever seen, and she enjoys the most screen time, though every female here is as sexy as any American star. Decidedly French, this film does have its odd side: the dwarf, a scene in robes and masks, and some misogynist dialogue, but the French are known as lovers for a damn good reason, and this film shows us why. *Vive!*

R & R

VCA Platinum. DIRECTOR: *Stuart Cantabury.* CAST: *Asia Carrera, Tyffany Mynx, Tricia Yen, Victoria Andrews, Melanie Maglow, Vivian, Tony Tedeschi, Buck Adams, Sean Michaels, Steve Drake*

I'm ambivalent about this tape. I was immediately fascinated by the use of Vietnam War–era combat news footage, but I was equally turned off by the weak acting and fake-looking sets throughout much of the movie. And yet . . .

Tony Tedeschi plays a soldier who has spent ten months in Vietnam remaining faithful to his girlfriend back home. The R and R of the title refers to the soldiers' relaxation time spent in a small, seedy bar near their encampment. All the guys are having their way with the bar girls in this establishment, except Tony, who sticks to beer and watching the antics of those around him. His buddy, Sean Michaels, as well as his nemesis, Buck Adams, playing a despicable lieutenant, drink and play in the bar.

The story is told in voice-over by Tony as he lies wounded in the dark while on a one-man recon mission. Explosives burst in the darkness as he tries to reach his base on the radio and as he remembers his past. Stock war footage is laced throughout his reminiscences.

After five weeks of not hearing from the girl back home, thinking he has been dumped, he succumbs to the beauty of Asia Carrera. Afterward, he learns that his mail has been delivered to the wrong company. Distraught over what he has done, he leaves for the recon mission where he is badly wounded.

Tony lies on the hillside in the dawn, and, in a vision, his girlfriend from home walks toward him, helps him to his feet, tells him she's not mad at him, and leads him away. In the distance they literally disappear.

The camera pans back to the hillside. Tony is still lying there. He dies.

Not your standard erotic film ending. Even though I found much of this tape off-putting, I found myself moved by the ending. Curious.

Two highlights are the sex scene between Tony and Asia Carrera, whom I find one of the most striking women in the business. She's Asian, as the name implies, and has a lovely, all-natural body, smooth skin, and no gargantuan implants.

The other highlight is Sean Michaels' scene with Tricia Yen. Michaels is a real force of nature: large in every respect. His 17-minute pairing with this tiny woman is a real study in contrasts and the adaptability of the female body.

I give this one a go, even with all the caveats outlined above.

THE REEL WORLD

Forbidden Films.   DIRECTOR: *Frank Marian.*   CAST: *Christina Angel, Lacey Rose, Dyanna Lauren, Lana Sands, Alex Sanders, Gerry Pike, Nick East, Mickey Ray*

If you like the MTV show *The Real World*, where a group of twenty-somethings live together in a house and are under video scrutiny twenty four hours a day, you'll like this takeoff tape. Each of the cast plays the part of one of the familiar Real people—the spacey surfer, the semi-angry black chick, the really together older guy, etc., then they all have sex with each other in various combinations.

The talk-to-the-camera style of the MTV show works really well here, with some of the performers being able to handle their roles better than others.

I would like to recommend Lacey Rose, who goes nuts while having sex with Nick East. If this was mainstream acting, then get out the awards, because we'd have a winner. Now I'm going to get a little graphic here, but when she said, "Spit on my pussy," to Nick East, it sent a bolt of electricity through me that I'll take to my grave.

On the other hand, Gerry Pike, not my favorite anyway, acts so weird that you want to step into his Reel World and hit him over the head with an ashtray. But he's only in one scene and Lacey Rose is in two, so that tips the scales in favor of the tape.

And I didn't even mention Mickey Ray dumping powdered sugar on Lana Sands and licking it off.

SEAN MICHAELS IS THE MAN WHO LOVES WOMEN

VCA Pictures Platinum. DIRECTOR: *Sean Michaels and Thomas Stone.* CAST: *Sean Michaels, Tara Monroe, Janet Jacme, Ariel Day, Wednesday, Lana Sands, Peter North, Tom Byron*

This is one of the first interracial videos Beth and I watched together, and if you're unfamiliar with the genre, Sean Michaels is the best actor to start with. He's tall, dark, handsome, and very well hung. Sean has a nice shy acting style, is by far the most stylish actor in the industry, and is a superior lover.

The Man Who Loves Women is shot as a documentary of a typical Hollywood day in Sean Michaels' life. A cameraman follows him around as he picks up women and tapes their lovemaking. This *cinema verité* style is very erotic when it's believable; unfortunately, the premise is undercut by several lapses in verisimilitude.

The first scene finds Sean helping a woman, Tara Monroe, who is trying on a dress in a clothing shop. The flirtation between Tara and Sean is sexy, and his seduction of her is very realistic. Seeing the diminutive Tara perform with the towering Sean is most erotic.

Sean is then recognized on the street by a fan, Ariel Day, who invites him back to her place. This scene seems accidental, until they arrive at her apartment—where the cameraman is already waiting! Memo to the directors: If you're going to film a documentary, at least film it correctly. This seems to be the first in a series, so let's hope they come to understand the genre.

Tara and Wednesday call Sean and invite him for a threesome. I especially liked Wednesday's pierced tongue. Not something that Beth is going to do anytime in the near future, but maybe when we're older and the kids are in college.

Another scene with Janet Jacme, Sean, and Tom Byron is ruined by the fact that Byron has become such a grungy dude. A shave, shower, and haircut would greatly improve his sex appeal.

The final scene, a ménage à trois with Sean, Peter North, and Lana Sands ends the video on a sexy note. North's cum shot is, of course, prodigious and messy, but the performers seem to enjoy it. Sean ends the video with a promise of more to come. Let's hope he keeps it.

THE SECRET GARDEN (PARTS ONE AND TWO)

X-Citement. DIRECTOR: *Michael Zen.* CAST: *Ashlyn Gere, Ona Zee, Randy Spears, Mike Horner, Flame, Jonathan Morgan, P. J. Sparxx, T. T. Boy, Anisa, Nikki Sinn, Tom Chapman, Melanie Moore*

This film opens with Ona Zee masturbating against a giant stone phallus in a garden, and never makes much more sense thereafter. The plot has something to do with a family and its secrets, and a woman who threatens to expose them. This is one of those situations where even though they spent more money, they didn't necessarily make a better film. The sex scenes are erotic enough, but the story doesn't really gel. An early scene features T. T. Boy and P. J. Sparxx having sex. During this scene the camera crew is revealed. Turns out they're filming a movie, produced by banker Mike Horner (this is his secret), who is seduced by Ashlyn Gere in a blond wig.

Randy Spears, Horner's son, has a secret—he likes watching erotic movies. He views a scene of T. T. Boy and Anisa in a movie booth, then picks up a hitchhiker, Ashlyn Gere, this time in a redhead wig. This scene is stimulating, although Randy irritatingly addresses the camera several times.

Ona Zee's character, Horner's wife, apparently has a thing for gloves, as she receives a shipment of gloves in the mail, which induces her to masturbate. The giant stone phallus again makes an appearance, for no reason.

Flame, Randy's wife, receives a phone call saying that Randy has been cheating on her, so she has sex with Randy and plays a fantasy game as a hooker.

Jonathan Morgan arrives with his new fiancée, who turns out to be Ashlyn Gere. Part one ends here.

THE SECRET GARDEN, PART TWO

The sequel opens with Jonathan and Ashlyn discussing the family. They do have a sex scene together, but where does Ashlyn get the nurse's uniform? Is she really supposed to be the nurse who seduced Jonathan years before? Next is a flashback fantasy sequence where Ashlyn watches her mother, Nikki Sinn, have an affair with Tom Chapman, who is supposed to be Mike Horner's brother. Ashlyn's father kills himself over the affair and Horner's family takes over the house and business. Ashlyn's mother tells her to seek revenge by revealing the family's secrets.

Ashlyn and Randy have another nice scene together in the bathroom, then Ashlyn seduces Flame before they're caught by Ona Zee. Fade to a sex scene with Ona and Mike Horner. Fade back to the earlier scene, where Ona kills Ashlyn and buries her in the flower garden.

Confused? So were we. I always enjoy Ashlyn's tapes, and these are good-looking videos with many arousing sex scenes, but they can't overcome such a poorly written script. Here's the deal: Sometimes you go to the tape store and all the good ones we recommend are gone. Rent this one instead.

SEX

VCA-Platinum. DIRECTOR: *Michael Ninn.* CAST: *Sunset Thomas, Gerry Pike, Tyffany Million, Ritchie Razor, Chasey Lane, Jon Dough, Debi Diamond, Misty Rain, Diva, Asia Carrera, Deidre Holland*

This is one of the big kahunas of recent adult films. A VCA-Platinum film, it came out in 1994, eagerly awaited and much ballyhooed. It is directed by Michael Ninn and stars many of the mainstream adult performers you'll see over and over in these tapes, all of them fine-looking people and a pleasure to watch. The film was nominated for nineteen separate awards in the 1995 Adult Video News Awards, won nine, and deserved more.

This is one of the tapes with a heavy plot, or at least heavy for adult films. It's the old rags-to-riches-to-rags story of a man brought low by his lust for stardom.

There are some very lush production values here with enough high-quality camera work (dissolves, unusual angles) to push it almost into the art film category. The sets are extremely modern with a sort of elegant minimalist look that contrasts nicely with the concept of naked people having sex within them.

One of the featured scenes is a long dream sequence involving a futuristic stack of video screens on a bare stage—the women are all wearing look-alike Cleopatra wigs, which is fairly wacky, but the style level is extremely high. There is something mildly hallucinogenic about this scene that appeals more to a sense of dance than sexual interest.

The male star, Gerry Pike, is a long-haired pretty boy, which is fine with me. He's not one of my favorite performers, but he does a credible job in this tape. He is a more proficient actor than many erotic video stars, and since this is a story-heavy film he must draw on this side of his talent more than these performers usually do. He also has an accent that Beth finds intriguing.

It also stars Jon Dough, one of the stalwarts of the field, who towards the end delivers several very long speeches carrying the moral of the movie, which seems to be Don't Get Too Big For Your Britches Or You'll Get Depressed And Try To Kill Yourself And Have An Out-Of-Body Sex Scene And End Up Back In The Desert Where You Started From Only Now You're An Old Man.

It doesn't really matter much what it's about. The fact that it has any story at all is a plus, and coupled with the high production values and beautiful people, VCA has come up with an excellent example of the genre. This film would be a fine place for many couples who are interested in erotic videos to begin.

Sex II: Fate

VCA Platinum. Director: *Michael Ninn.* Cast: *Sunset Thomas, Tyffany Million, Debi Diamond, Deidre Holland, Shayla Laveaux, Chasey Lane, Diva, Misty Rain, Asia Carrera, Gerry Pike, Jon Dough, Steve Drake, Ritchie Razor, Zachery Addams*

Sex II: Fate is, of course, the sequel to Ninn's *Sex*, and tells the story of Sunset Thomas' rise and fall as a sex symbol as she searches for her true love, Gerry Pike.

As usual in a Ninn film, the storyline is hard as hell to follow, but the filmaking and sex are phenomenal. The Charles Bukowskiesque narration does little to explain the plot, but it does sound cool. The film includes scenes from *Sex* that make no sense if you haven't already seen it, but the scenes are arousing, so who cares? It's sometimes hard to tell who's having sex and why, but the high style and quick, seamless editing make the watching worthwhile. The rewind and slow-motion buttons get a real workout on Ninn films.

All the scenes are worth viewing—though there's one brief disconcerting shot of Jon Dough receiving offscreen fellatio from Pike that is the first blatantly homoerotic scene I've witnessed in straight erotica—and I especially liked a Sunset Thomas–Steve Drake episode. Beth really enjoys the costumes in Ninn films, the rubber and latex gear that are almost impossible to wear in real life, but damn sexy on-screen. The moral of the sequel is almost the same as the first, that fame, particularly sexual fame, thoroughly corrupts, and Pike rejects Sunset when she returns to his gas station a star. If you're in the mood for stylish sex, you can't beat one of these two films. A fine prelude to an evening's entertainment for any couple. It was for us.

SEX LIVES OF CLOWNS

VCA Platinum Plus. DIRECTOR: *Wesley Emerson.* CAST: *Kaitlyn Ashley, Jeanna Fine, Crystal Wilder, Sarah Jane Hamilton, Debi Diamond, Nicole London, Brooke Waters, Jon Dough, Jonathan Morgan, Mike Horner, Cal Jammer, Dave Hardman*

Who thinks up these plots? Someone demented came up with this one and we should all be grateful. This is a very funny tape.

Sarah Jane Hamilton is a therapist interviewing a series of clowns and clown groupies. The tape opens with a tracking shot of Jon Dough jogging, talking about being a clown and what a tough life it is. A curious clop-clop sound is heard throughout. The camera pulls back and we see he is jogging in clown shoes.

A commentator comes on screen and tells us that it's not all fun and games being a clown, that in fact a clown's life is generally one of quiet desperation and bitter disappointment. We cut to Jonathan Morgan being interviewed by Sarah Jane and once again we see why I think he's the best male actor in the adult business. This time he does a comic routine with a tube sock he calls Senor Paco, then he has a sex scene with a lady whom Senor Paco chases around for awhile before getting down to business.

Mike Horner then does a sex scene as a clown who can only be turned on by calliope music. Very strange.

In fact the whole tape is strange and funny. The least interesting parts are the sex scenes. It suffers from that shot-on-tape malady—too much clarity. The ladies need to guard more carefully against razor burn and the close-ups are way too close up, and the inflated breasts are too damn big, and when they stop the calliope music they substitute the usual boring synth stuff, whereas although the calliope was weird, it was much better. But the premise and the short bits are so funny I have to give it a hearty recommendation even with the usual pitfalls.

And if you haven't seen Sarah Jane do her squirt trick, this has got a good one, besides what I thought were several other genuine female orgasms. All in all a solid rental if you want a lot of laughs along with your sex.

SEX TOURS OF HONG KONG

Astral Ocean. DIRECTOR: *None credited.* CAST: *Asian and European actors and actresses*

I had to rent this tape, even though I thought it was going to be pretty bad. I have a *National Geographic* interest in these tapes—remember, many of them have almost no plot or *inherent* value other than the sex—so I like to see the people and places of foreign lands while I'm getting the sex. Besides, there's always the chance that these foreigners will have some new and really different way of doing what is essentially pretty much the same series of moves the world over. So far this has not been the case, though I have seen some very lovely scenery.

But the real reason I rented the tape was the ad copy on the box. There were the usual pictures of naked women, all Asian in this case, but below the pictures were these claims:

Stunning Females!
Asian Masturbation!
Chinese Love Motel Sex!
The Clearest Close-ups!
Blow Jobs in Cars!
Sex with Tourists!
Interracial Lust!
Bottoms Drilled Graphically!

So I rented it, thinking that the fractured English on the box might somehow transfer into a few laughs on the tape, but no such luck. There were some nice shots of Hong Kong, and they did fulfill all their claims, but unless your thing is Asian folks (except for the German tourist) going at it *real close up*, I wouldn't waste my money.

But reviewing this tape allows me to drag up my soap box and spend a minute puffing the American sex film industry. We may have lost the silicon war to the Japanese (I could make a few implant jokes here, but I'll spare you), the Germans might be models of economic stability, and yes, the French have better food, but when it comes to good-looking erotic stars and high production values, the United States rules the world. If for no other reason than our advanced dentistry, our stars are heads, shoulders, and teeth above all others.

In my European tape–viewing experience, the German women are pale and dumpy, the men Nazi-like; the French have a lean, feral cast, especially the guys; the English have pale skin and really big bottoms; the Scandinavians are good-looking but appear bored, bored, bored with the whole process; and the Eastern Europeans, the former Communists, well, they really should do something about all those serious skin rashes.

Suffice it to say, this is one area where it really makes sense to Buy American.

SILK STOCKINGS (THE BLACK WIDOW)

Sterling Pictures. DIRECTORS: *Geraldine Greystoke and Greg Steelberg.*
CAST: *Tyffany Million, Jenna Jameson, Tyffany Mynx, Nikole Lace,
Barbara Doll, Olivia, Jordan Lee, Steven St. Croix, Bobby Vitale, Vince
Voyeur, Tom Byron, Steve Drake, E. Z. Ryder*

This is a mystery story with Tyffany Million as a femme fatale
who frames bartender Steven St. Croix for the death of her
nightclub-owner husband, E. Z. Ryder (in a nonsexual role).

The color and sound of the video are not top quality, but the
movie does try to keep from being a complete *Body Heat* rip-off.
The actors perform well in both the speaking and sexual scenes,
and a credible attempt has been made to meld a mystery with
sex. St. Croix does wear black socks during his first scene with
Million, but, as the scene takes place in a dingy storeroom and
the sex is well done, Beth let it slide.

Million personifies the evil, seductive woman who uses sex to
lead a man down a dark path. Tom Byron, as a small-time bookie
who becomes a dead body double for E. Z. Ryder, has a nice
scene in a limo, ending in a particularly wet orgasm from Byron.
There's a very nice foursome, with each of three girls. The sexy
flirtation between detective Steve Drake and Million adds to the
thrill of their act.

The final twist to the mystery isn't too clever, but if you
wanted a tough case to crack, you'd be reading Agatha Christie.
If you want steamy sex surrounded by a plausible story, *Silk
Stockings* makes for a good erotic mystery film.

SINDERELLA: PART ONE

Vivid Film. DIRECTOR: *Paul Thomas.* CAST: *Savannah, Racquel
Darrian, Brit Morgan, P. J. Sparxx, Melanie Moore, Randy Spears, Joey
Silvera, Randy West, T. T. Boy, Mike Horner*

Restoration comedy in full dress. And undress. A big-budget
production.

The film opens with the credits projected over a close-up of two ladybugs locked in mating embrace as they wander over a leafy garden. Surely a first in erotic films: bug sex!

Mother Goose then appears and tells us we are about to see the story of Sinderella. Mother Goose continues to tell the story in voice-over and to supply continuity when there are extreme scene changes.

We open with Mike Horner strolling the garden path, strumming a mandolin and singing. Probably another first. In the background, Sinderella is making love to T. T. Boy. A chamber music sound track takes over from Horner.

Horner, as Lord Essex, is having dinner with Sinderella, the new Mrs. Essex, and her two evil daughters. Death appears at the door and asks for Horner, who then dies. He didn't even get a sex scene in this movie. Amazing.

As expected, the evil stepmother and the daughters do dastardly things to poor Sinderella. Sinderella remains cheerful, though.

Joey Silvera is an armor salesman. He helps Sinderella scrub the staircase. I was waiting for a standard silly staircase sex scene, and when there wasn't one I found myself mildly annoyed. This just goes to show you how your expectations can be shaped by watching these movies.

Joey Silvera is making a new suit of armor for Randy West, the prince's right-hand man. Randy says he can get the Essex family invited to the ball, but he has to sleep with all the girls first. Kind of a royal food taster sort of thing.

So he does. Here the classical music sound track switches to jazz. Why? Who knows, but it works just fine.

Meanwhile, Joey has Sinderella.

The night of the big ball, the stepmother and sisters depart, leaving Sinderella behind. Her fairy godmother finally shows up and they begin the task of outfitting Sinderella.

Meanwhile, the ball is proceeding with everyone in court dress, drinking champagne and eating Oreos and Fig Newtons. Perhaps a few more bucks could have been thrown at the hors d'oeuvres, but I guess it was part of the comedy.

People at the ball have sex, and then suddenly the tape ends. They show us scenes from part two, which look a lot like scenes from part one.

As yet we've not located a copy of part two, but that's okay, we get the idea and we know how it's going to end anyway. They did mention that the bit with the glass slipper fitting the right foot is not part of this plot; instead, it's whether some other member fits a certain someplace.

This is a mildly clever movie with some mildly clever dialogue based on a mildly clever premise. If you're in the mood for blazing sex, don't rent it, but if a mildly clever diversion is enough, you can't go far wrong.

We'll keep looking for part two.

THE SWAP

Vivid. DIRECTOR: *Paul Thomas.* CAST: *Jennifer Stewart, Sharon Kane, Madison, Paula Price, Heather St. Clair, Bridgette Monroe, Jerry Butler, Joe Schultz, Eric Price, Tom Byron, Axel Horn, Max Steel, Lance Carrington*

I liked *The Swap II* better (see following review), but Beth preferred this one. Jennifer Stewart and Joe Schultz want to have children, but can't. Their scene opens up with Stewart taking her vaginal temperature in the proper, legs-up position. Someone did their homework on this one.

Eventually they decide to ask the help of their best friends and business partners to rectify the situation. Along the way they are reluctantly involved in an orgy at Madison's house and have various scenes of sex among themselves.

Unlike *The Big Chill*, the partner swapping is not embraced by all the partners, and an unfortunate freeze occurs between the men friends. This is finally resolved and everyone becomes best pals again.

Because of the "serious" use of the infertility subject matter, this one has the feel of the older films from the Golden Age.

While it seemed a little thin to me, the feminine half of the reviewing team gave it a solid recommendation, again, because of the subject. Enough said.

THE SWAP II

Vivid. DIRECTOR: *Paul Thomas.* CAST: *Lene, Lenna, Jon Dough, Marc Wallice, Dyanna Lauren, Tony Tedeschi, Misty Rain, Alex Sanders, Isis Nile, Brad Armstrong, Asia Carrera, Chad Thomas, Christina Angel, Damien Zeus, Veronica Sage*

I must confess that I find Lene an extremely attractive performer. Maybe it's her slight overbite, or maybe it's her butt. I don't know, but for me she's a real turn-on.

Even though this is titled *Part II*, it's not a sequel. In the very beginning the two women, Lene and Lenna (*that* must have been confusing on the set), mumble something about having tried it once but never again, and that's the end of any connection to *Swap I*.

It begins very cleverly. The two couples, Lene and Dough and Lenna and Wallice, are gathered together for an evening of Chinese food and talk. The gag is that you can't tell who is married to whom. The two couples are mismatched in that Dough is more like Lenna, and Wallice like Lene, both in their sexual styles and dinner choices.

It seems that both Dough and Lenna want their respective mates to join them in a visit to a local sex club. Lene rejects this suggestion and storms off to the bedroom. Dough follows her to make amends. In the living room, Lenna begins seducing Wallice, who thinks the time and place inappropriate, but can't withstand his wife's charms. Meanwhile, Lene is sulking in the bathroom and Dough seduces her there.

This leads me to an aside. Next to staircases, these directors seem to prefer bathrooms as a sex site. While I don't find them objectionable, Beth always winces as the poor ladies are, ahem, laid on the cold marble countertops, heads banging into various perfumes and sundries. This scene is no exception, though the two lovers do eventually decide to remove themselves to the bedroom. Where they are observed by Lenna and Wallice from the doorway, involved in their own session. I found this a very steamy scene. Beth liked it as well, once Lene got her head out of the toiletries.

At any rate, Dough and Lenna depart for the local sex club. I recommend fast-forwarding through this whole next orgy sequence. These scenes are usually dull, with the less attractive performers assigned to this group role. Dough and Lenna watch, and then join in the action in various combinations.

Back at the house, Wallice seduces Lene to get back at their erring partners. Another great scene. Maybe it's just my attraction to Lene, but I swear the girl has an actual on-screen orgasm.

Eventually Jon Dough comes home repentant, and Wallice leaves to search for his wife, who has gone on to yet another sex party.

TANGLED

Pleasure Productions. DIRECTOR: *Mike Horner.* CAST: *Mike Horner, Tyffany Million, Nina Hartley, Ona Zee, Devon Shire, Jessie Eastern, Tony Tedeschi, Ariana, Tina Tedeschi*

This is a very clever film. It seems to be a fable with a message, though I wasn't able to figure out what the message was supposed to be. No matter.

Mike Horner appears at the very beginning, naked, wrapped in the sort of large net big-game hunters used to catch lions with. He rolls around on the ground in the net for a while as the credits roll by.

The film is broken up into four acts.

Act I: Just Folks

Mike is sitting on the ground in a field, wrapped in his net. Still naked. A vintage Cadillac pulls up and out hops Tyffany

Million and a guy who looks just like the fellow who used to be on *Starsky and Hutch*. The blond one. Beth says it isn't him, but she agrees that it does look like him.

She (Tyffany, not Beth) is dressed in a fifties-type pink dress, with period hairdo to match. He's wearing a white shirt, suspenders, and black slacks.

Mike asks for help. He needs to be freed. Tyffany and the guy are very sympathetic, but they can't figure out any way to assist him. This is the theme of the movie. Everyone is sympathetic and would like to help, but no one seems to know quite how to go about it. Besides, they say, he got himself into this mess, he ought to be able to figure his way out of it. The humor is, of course, he could simply pull off the net, but doesn't.

Believe me, it's a lot more clever than I'm making it sound.

At any rate, Tyffany blathers on about what a nice spot this would be to build a house and start a family. They decide to start the family right then and there. She brings out a picnic lunch and Mike eats crackers while Tyffany and her man, whom she calls Daddy, make love. It's all quite idyllic.

A word about the music. Music in these movies is usually terrible: synthesized rock, keyboard nothingness, bland and boring. The music and sound in this movie are terrific.

As is the acting. I am always amazed when a director and writer give these people lines that aren't incredibly stupid and scenes where they can show that they really can act. Everyone does a very credible job.

Tyffany and Daddy get back in the car and drive off. Mike is still in his net.

Act II: The Virgin.

A young girl rides up on her bicycle. Not really a young girl, but that's the impression they give us. Horner says, "I'm all tangled up here. I'm in a bit of a bind." He asks for help, but she doesn't give him any. She realizes that he's helpless, so she sits in front of him and masturbates. Then she gets up and rides off on her bike.

Then she rides back. She says she knows that was a nasty

thing to do to him, but she's a virgin. He's a virgin as well. She offers to have sex with him. They do, with the net draped over them both.

Act III: Sex Kitten and Other Friends.

Night. A car drives up. A guy and two girls. The fellow is dressed like Alex in *A Clockwork Orange* and the girls are in sexy outfits. This viewer feared the plot was about to veer into mayhem, but it didn't. Out of the car climb about thirty more people of all sizes and descriptions. Many are dressed like hippies. They light a campfire and begin a big dance scene that becomes a large orgy. Meanwhile, Mike is still in his net, although several girls are having sex with him.

Act IV: A Relationship

Morning. Mike wakes up alone. He gets up and begin walking, still naked, still in his net. He walks over hills, through dales, up mountains, through creeks. Night follows day, follows night, follows day. Exhausted, he sits by a lovely creek. The grass rustles, and a voice says, "Ahem, I've been looking for you." Out of the high grass crawls a naked woman, wrapped in a net.

They attempt to untangle each other, but can't. They talk, then make love. In the morning they get up, still netted, and walk off, hand in hand.

I think all of this is a metaphor for relationships in general, and maybe even about the trap of being an actor in these types of films. But then again, maybe it wasn't.

Whatever it is, I think it's a terrific film.

THINGS CHANGE: MY FIRST TIME

Cal Vista. DIRECTOR: *Paul Thomas.* CAST: *Deidre Holland, Nikki Dial, Paula Harlow, Francesca Le, Flame, Woody Long, Mickey Ray, Jon Dough*

This is the first in a series of *Things Change* films from Paul Thomas, and like most films from actor-turned-directors, it is strong on performances, both sexual and otherwise. Deidre Holland and

Nikki Dial portray lovers whose relationship changes when Nikki leaves to explore her heterosexual side. Same-sex partnerings in erotic videos seldom offer more than mere titillation, but here you can believe these women are in a relationship, and the emotions and lovemaking they portray are believable and sexy.

More of a first-in-a-series than a stand-alone film, this video is mostly plotless, with each sex scene another exploration of Nikki's character's sexuality, but the motivations and performances are credible enough to keep you watching. Every scene is a standout, sexually, but I particularly liked Deidre and Nikki's lovemaking together and Nikki masturbating in the shower. If you're in the mood for sexy soap opera, *Things Change* is a series worth looking into.

VELVET

Sterling Pictures. DIRECTOR: *Geoffry Coldwater*. CAST: *Jeanna Fine, Kristy Waay, Nikki Sinn, Nena Anderson, Cassie Williams, Tabitha Stevens, Mike Horner, Dick Nasty, Slave Dave, J. P. Ronnocco, Hank Rose*

This is a One Day in the Life of a Hooker type of tape. Jeanna Fine is the hooker and she looks very good in the role. (Jeanna Fine is better in her short hair roles than she is in her earlier, long hair days.)

Her husband doesn't seem to realize what her job is when he heads off to work. The sex at night is dull. But during the day, Jeanna swings.

One of the oddities of this film is that there's no dialogue between any of the characters. None. The only spoken words come from a gag that runs off and on throughout the film where a weird weather lady gives weird weather on a television that's always on somewhere in the scene. (The wacky weather lady is played by Hustler Erotic magazine columnist Whally Wharton. This is an inside joke.)

I'm recommending this one to any of you specialty viewers out there—it starts off with an S&M scene between Jeanna and a cast member who could only be Slave Dave, as credited in the titles. Jeanna does Dave, who is bound and gagged with a red rubber ball, with a hefty strap-on dildo. This is pretty unusual in these tapes, and while it isn't to my taste at all, I figure there must be a certain percentage of readers and viewers who might like this sort of thing. So here it is.

The rest of the sex is pretty vanilla, though there's a definite antimale agenda that I couldn't quite put my finger on.

Rent it at your discretion, but for those who like the occasional oddity, this will fit the bill nicely.

Beth hates it when I bring home weird tapes like this.

Chapter 7

One After Another: Series Tapes

*T*here are many series tapes. These seldom have much of a story and are usually of interest mostly to your single-guy viewer. We thought we'd review some of them so you'd know what to stay away from, or what to go to if you're interested in their premise.

We don't like most series tapes, but there are exceptions. After you've seen a number of these tapes you might find yourself branching out and watching for reasons other than story. Or let's just say that you don't always have to have a story. In this category I put the tapes that are shot in unusual, at least to me, locations. I like to look at the scenery, as well as the sex. This is the same impulse that leads me, when the shooting takes place inside someone's home, to try and read the covers of the books on the bookshelves.

So here are a few that I liked because of the exotic scenery. I watch a lot of *National Geographic* specials as well.

THE BUTTMAN TAPES

There's a bunch of them. Buttman (John Stagliano) goes to Rio a number of times, Buttman goes to England, Buttman goes to various other countries. They're all the same, and if you're like me and like to look at the local scenery, you may enjoy a few of them, but in general they're not couple's material.

In fact, we called Stagliano's company, Evil Angel, and asked them if they wanted to submit some films that they thought would interest couples. They decided not to submit anything. Stagliano was not really interested in couples, they said, though he "worshipped women." Fair enough. We agree.

But we *do* recommend two Stagliano films, *Face Dance I* and *II*, which show that he is also a funny, intelligent, talented director when he's not just doing his Buttman thing.

BUTTMAN GOES TO RIO III AND IV

Evil Angel. DIRECTOR: *John "Buttman" Stagliano.* CAST: *Tianna, Priscila, Doda, Luciana, Honey, Rocco Sefreddi, Felipe, Joey Silvera*

I've always wanted to go to Rio. You see pictures of the fabulous beaches and the fabulous people, but still pictures don't really do justice to the scenery. The women on these beaches are terrific. The bathing suits are tiny and amazing. Nowhere in America, at least on a public beach, do you see such expanses of lovely flesh. Buttman goes to the beach and really delivers.

Unfortunately, once there, he and his pals act like idiots, peeking around, giggling, pointing, and whispering. "Look! Look at that ass! Oh my God, look at those tits!" They sound like they're fourteen years old.

But that doesn't seem to stop them from picking up women and taking them back to the hotel room.

I'll describe *Rio IV* as I saw that one most recently, but the scenery is pretty much the same in all of the *Rio* tapes.

The gimmick here is that Buttman is back in Rio and he's

brought Rocco, his main man, and also Joey Silvera. Joey is a tall, normal-looking guy. The gag is that Joey hasn't been able to get laid in Rio. Rocco keeps making humorous disparaging remarks about Joey, as if he doesn't know him.

Another in this cast of Lost Boys is Felipe, who's a muscular Brazilian guy who Beth says is "cute, in a Sly Stallone sort of way."

In the Rio series, Buttman and the boys hit the beach and look at the girls. Then they single one out, or in the case of *Rio III*, two, and Felipe takes them to the hotel room where they have sex.

The idea is that these girls are not adult film stars, but just ordinary women. While I don't particularly believe it, for the most part they're not shaved and shorn like all American adult stars, and they have the breasts God gave them, which is a nice change these days.

In *Rio IV* Felipe picks up a beautiful but unusual-looking woman. She seems to have Indian blood, and she is very fuzzy. All over. The boys think that is pretty great, and so did I.

One of the turnoffs for me is that Buttman continues to talk to Felipe as Felipe is making love to the woman. They discuss how great she is, how hot, how much she's enjoying it. This breaks the mood for me, but others might not mind their chatter.

Another thing I don't like is Buttman's insistence on the gynecological close-ups. And I mean close up. What's the point?

The boys go on a sightseeing jaunt on a funicular railway to the top of Sugarloaf Mountain, a Rio landmark. They are joined by a blonde, who I think is Buttwoman, but they never really say. There they follow a woman and her boyfriend until the boyfriend leaves and then the two ladies have sex in the outdoors. This scene is unusual in that it includes that rare beast, a genuine female orgasm.

Back at the beach, it's raining. This doesn't stop Rocco from picking up a girl and taking her back to the room and doing his patented Rocco Sefreddi number on her. All the time chatting with Buttman.

Finally, the sun is shining again and our trio of boys is back on the beach where Rocco takes pity on Joey and picks up a girl for him. She's a stunner, reddish-blond hair and wonderful freckled skin. They go back to her place (small, but with a great view of the beach) and make love. Buttman keeps his mouth shut, for the most part, through this one.

Rio III features a long sequence shot in a nightclub which gives you a good look at many female butts as they dance around. Rocco picks up a girl and they go back to the hotel. Other than this nightclub scene, all is much the same as in *Rio IV*.

While I can't give the Buttman my wholehearted recommendation, he at least provides some interesting diversion in a genre that can use some diversification. If you've watched a number of the more plot-driven films and want something different, you might give Buttman a try. Beth can't watch him for long because of the camera work. Buttman uses a handheld videocamera, which makes for some vertiginous swings and pans, and gives Beth motion sickness. Oh, well, it's more of a guy's thing anyway.

MAX HARDCORE

Xplor. DIRECTOR: *Max Steiner*

Max Hardcore's thing is to find amateur women to have anal sex with and do it in a semibrutal manner. It disgusted us. I know the women aren't coerced, I know they don't appear harmed or in most cases even in pain, but it is still a turnoff.

Ed Powers: Dirty Debutantes, and Others

4-Play Video. DIRECTOR: *Ed Powers*

Ed Powers is a very ordinary looking guy who has parlayed an extremely simple idea into a very big and probably lucrative business. In the early days, Ed and another guy were known as The Nasty Brothers. Their shtick was to invite women into their home, basement, apartment, whatever, and then have sex with them on-camera. Some of the women bring boyfriends who appear on-camera with them, but most of them just have sex with Ed. These women are supposed to be video-sex newcomers, hence the Debutantes of the title, and though some professionals sneak in, most of them do indeed seem to be video virgins.

It's amazing how many women actually sign on to this project. Most of them do it seemingly because they are interested in getting into the adult film business. And many of them have. It's possible to look at early Ed Powers tapes and find first timers who went on to the Big Show.

There are more than forty tapes in the *Debutante* series, and Powers has spun off the concept into a number of other series.

We don't really like the *Debutante* series. To put it bluntly, the main problem is Mr. Powers. In the early tapes he was kind of fat, but he started working out and his body got better. But he still looks like just a regular guy. He's losing his hair, which he keeps in a pony tail, he's *extremely* pale, he often keeps his black socks on, and he always keeps his glasses on. The women are always better looking than Ed. Female viewers won't get any kind of a kick out of watching Ed do it.

The thing is, Ed's intelligent and sometimes a pretty funny guy. His modus operandi is to spend some time taping the girl in an extended question and answer period. This is actually the most interesting part of these tapes. Sometimes it's funny, even intentionally so, often it's sad. Sometimes the girls are of limited intelligence, and sometimes they look stoned or drunk, though everyone in the industry says that Ed never resorts to such methods. I believe it. There seem to be plenty of women willing to line up for Ed's attention without coercion of any kind.

Sometimes the women are absolutely beautiful, and it's then that I find myself shouting at the screen during the interview, "No, don't do it! You don't need to sleep with Ed! It's not worth it!"

But they never hear me, and they almost always sleep with Ed.

I don't blame Ed; he's obviously got something that lots of women want, and he's probably living out some dream fantasy of a lifetime. But I'm not going to recommend his tapes.

PRIVATE

Private is a European company that makes and distributes their own films.

Another of the "exotic locale" series is produced by Private. I'll review several of the ones I liked, or at least thought had interesting parts, though there are others which we have seen which we didn't like at all. There were no bad or disgusting parts in the ones we didn't like, we just found them silly or boring.

Most of these tapes seem to feature mostly, at least to me, unknowns. A group of professionals go to a foreign location and round up some local talent to participate. The men usually look like guys who are on vacation and have fallen into a male fantasy. Most of the participants are European, interacting with whatever indigenous people live wherever they are shooting.

We recommend several of the Private films, but for the most part we don't like them. We watched a bunch more, *The Tower I* and *II*, *Lady of Spain*, and some others and found them repetitive, not very well made, and in lots of instances, silly. If the scenery wasn't really spectacular (see *Lady of Spain* for some really dull Spanish vistas) then there wasn't any reason to watch them.

PRIVATE: CANNES FANTASIES

Private Video/Odyssey Group Video. DIRECTOR: *Frank Thring.*
CAST: *Kim, Angelica, Nathalie, Hannah, Roxanne, various men*

There's not a lot of story in these Private offerings, but there's
enough to hold the sex scenes together. We thought this one was
going to be about the Cannes Film Festival. It wasn't.

A group of actresses gather in a living room to tell each other
their private fantasies. This tape appealed to Beth, who I think
was more familiar with the concept of a bunch of women sitting
around telling each other stories.

But in this case, the fantasies are then acted out.

Kim, a Russian, fantasizes that she's a major movie star and
she's having sex on a balcony. She does so.

Angelica is an actress in an X-rated video. Nathalie wants to
be treated as a sex object, Hannah wants a great-looking guy and
a waterfall, and Roxanne is featured in a lace outfit and finds
three guys with a banana, whipped cream, and kiwifruit. These
multiple-partners scenes are a mainstay of the Private tapes. If
you don't like to see three men and one woman, don't rent any
of them. But none of these multiples is forced and everyone
looks like they're having a good time. Besides, isn't this a pretty
common fantasy for women as well as men?

PRIVATE: THE GOLDEN TRIANGLE

Private Video/Odyssey Group Video. DIRECTOR: *Jean-Paul Bouchet.*
CAST: *Su Ann, Gyanty, Rebecca, Linda, Lolita, Barbara, Marc, Frank
Vercase, Silvio, Alain Deloin, Alberto Ray.*

We had pretty much given up on Private tapes until we noticed
that Ann Grogan had recommended *Golden Triangle I* and *II* in
her Romantasy Video Recommendations (see our Resource section). So we thought we'd give this one a try.

Filmed on the island of Bali, there are lots of exterior shots of rain forests and temples and scenic inlets. Birds tweet in the dripping forest. Oh yeah, there's also lots of sex.

The story is some sort of drug-dealer nonsense with guys named The Ace of Spades and The Avenger, Italians and French mobsters, a Balinese Queen, and some guerrilla fighters. The saving grace is that the whole tape is in French so you don't have to bother much with the story. There's an English voice-over that fills you in, sort of, on the action. This voice-over is supplied by the female lead, who says things like, "After a mission, I always need a big hug." and "Silvio, like most Italians, has a big juicy dick instead of a brain." Fortunately, she doesn't talk all that much.

The ladies are all good-looking and the guys are all very southern European—swarthy, thin, hairy, intense. Beth says if you like men who look like this, it's a good tape, but if you don't, it isn't.

Did I mention the great scenery?

PRIVATE: SEYCHELLES

Private Video/Odyssey Group Video. DIRECTOR: *Michael Ricoud.* CAST: *Joey Silvera, Laura Catwoman, David Lecogneur, Stasha, Rob Terminator, Michaela, Karina, Christopher James, Valy Verdy, Sylvie, Jack Stricker, Sherazade, Fred Person*

I picked up this tape because the lovely woman on the cover looked like a naked version of one of the clerks down at my local convenience store. Kind of a strange reason, but sometimes we just have to follow our instincts. In this instance, it paid off.

As mentioned above, story is not the long suit in your standard Private tape. Here, the plot consists of writer Joey Silvera going somewhere private to write and then not getting laid like all the other guys do. (This seems to be a common theme in Joey's work.)

A whole bunch of people arrive on a boat at the Seychelles

islands. They then have sex with each other and some of the natives of the island. That's about it.

All of the women are very nice looking and the guys look like most of them were recruited on the dock, with the standard "Hey, guys, wanna be in a sex movie?" There was one German-looking fellow that Beth didn't like at all. I didn't like him much either.

Anyway, the woman who looks like the clerk at my convenience store was much in evidence, which was a real treat. She's the one pictured on the box cover, so if you like her looks, rent the tape because she's in it a lot.

Also, there's a tiny thing that happens that I found amazing. It goes by so quickly I missed it, but Beth caught it and I had to rewind to see it myself. I'll leave it a mystery for you. It occurs in one of the double penetration scenes (see glossary), of which Private filmmakers are so fond. It's with the French lady (Valy Verdy) and two guys on the beach. Look sharp.

The director, Michael Ricoud, was considered one of the tops in the business. Unfortunately, he died while making this movie. It seems he was standing on a rock directing one of the scenes, when a wave came up, knocked him over, and killed him. What a way to go.

I don't know if all of this adds up to a firm recommendation, but if you connect with the various elements I think you'll like it. Now excuse me, I've got to go down to the convenience store for a cup of coffee.

RANDY WEST'S UP AND CUMMERS

Erotica West/4-Play Video. DIRECTOR: *Randy West*

Randy West is a name, face, and body familiar to most adult film watchers. His career has continued from the Golden Age to today. He's good looking, a constant performer, and he can act. We recommend him in lots of movies in this book.

But we don't recommend his *Up and Cummers* series.

Randy is featured in many of Ed Powers' *Debutante* tapes. He's a lot easier to watch than Ed himself is. And he features himself in his own series.

The gimmick is the same as Ed's, except Randy appears on camera before and during the tape to explain who he has coming on and little details about the production. He shows the tapes of the women, whom he interviews pretty much the same as Ed does. Then he has sex with them or they have sex with someone they brought along, sometimes a man, sometimes another woman. Sometimes they don't have sex, just strip and show themselves.

Even though Randy is okay to watch, his stuff still has the same cheapo feel that Ed's tapes do. This is single-guy stuff, and unless your thing is watching Randy West, we say give it a pass.

Chapter 8

Amateur:
The Real Stuff

Usually you choose what amateur tapes you'd like to see by choosing a particular company, rather than the individual product. Each company seems to have a stable of performers who appear over and over, or a stable of performers who resemble each other in format and technique.

Homegrown Video

Homegrown has been in the business for thirteen years—starting out as a distributor of swinger tapes—which makes them real pioneers in the world of amateur video. They have more than 550 titles that span the gamut of legal sexuality.

They have a number of types of tapes, but most are just normal folks doing what comes naturally. Well, maybe not quite naturally.

The tapes are broken up into four or five scenes, the quality of which is indeed amateur. Rather than attempt to single out tapes that were really great, we just asked the company to send a sampling. Really, with a selection of 550 tapes, where do you start? Well, one place to start is with their sample tape, which has scenes from of a bunch of them. That might help, but there are still a lot of tapes to choose from.

435

How about that for a catchy title? *Number 435* kicked off with Vince La Rock and Tina going at it and having a lot of laughs while doing so. Vince is fiftyish, hairy, overweight, and refers to his penis as an Italian salami. Tina likes to be spanked.

Next up was Judy, a nice looking suburban lady in a solo scene with no sound. She utilizes a real arsenal of love weapons on herself, including one of the biggest dildos I have ever seen and a set of anal beads the size of unshucked walnuts. When she screws a set of C-clamps onto her nipples and tightens those babies down, I let out a scream that woke Beth from a deep and well-earned sleep.

Next a set of ordinary clothespins, painted black and hooked together with a small chain, took the place of the C-clamps. Ouch! I hit the fast-forward button.

Scene Number Three: Bob and Fran in a clever skit. Bob knocks on the door. Fran opens it. Bob says, "I've come for the rent!" Fran says she doesn't have any money. "We'll work something out," Bob says. They do.

That's enough. You get the idea.

There's a trailer at the end of the tape that says:

You can earn cash: send us your XXX home made videos. Get up to $15.00 per minute for your video. Call for info (800) 544-8144.

If you want to see your competition, rent some of Homegrown's videos. With a little planning, I'm sure you can earn some of that big cash.

There's really no way to review all of these movies. If you like the idea of amateur productions, order the catalogue (see

Resource section) and pick one out. If you like it, you'll like others. If you don't, you won't.

Pearl Necklace Video: Amorous Amateurs

The Amorous Amateurs series is amateur the way Double-A baseball teams are amateur ballplayers. They aren't, really. What we have here are Pro-Am tapes, which is not bad. On the contrary, you have the benefit of new or seldom-seen performers in productions that are higher level than the strictly amateurs.

45

Again, you get a series of scenes revolving around a situation, rather than a connecting story. In scene number one we have Lexus sitting on the bed in a silk negligee when there's a knock on the door. It's J. T., your friendly door-to-door sex toys salesman. J. T. comes in, spreads out his wares, and Lexus tries them out. Then she tries out J. T.

I've seen Lexus before in the big leagues. J. T. will probably never make it out of the farm team, but he's okay. The sex is well photographed and perfectly fine. Both Beth and I liked this one because there was lots of kissing and just general fondness between Lexus and J. T.

The next scenes were Amanda and Sean, John and Renee, and Jeff and Kriss. All were nice-looking and I didn't recognize any of the others. The situations weren't too silly and the sex believable. If you're looking for something in the Pro-Am line, these tapes are good.

TONYA HARDING'S HONEYMOON

Penthouse. DIRECTOR: *Tonya Harding and Jeff Gillooly.* CAST: *Tonya Harding, Jeff Gillooly*

Some of you have probably seen this on the shelves of your local video store. Don't bother with it. It is truly an amateur performance—the camera is sitting on a table, the lighting is bad, and at one point during sex the phone rings and *they answer it!* Tonya is not exactly a ball of fire. If it was Nancy Kerrigan maybe we'd give it a go, but as it is there's only the novelty value to recommend it. And not enough of that to make it worth the three bucks.

Video Alternatives

We discuss Video Alternatives in our chapter on resources. They are the biggest of the amateur suppliers.

Three videos we can recommend from Video Alternatives are *Heartland Honeys, Head Over Heels,* and *Ashley & Maria.*

HEARTLAND HONEYS

This video contains scenes featuring three different couples. In the first, a young twenty-something couple make love in a hotel room. She's blond, he's swarthy. The camerawork is often inept, but the girl is pretty and enthusiastic. This is a straightforward sex act, with no story offered or needed.

A second couple act out a fantasy. It's got a lot of great scenes, including a super scene of her masturbating. Unfortunately, it's also got a *looong* scene of him dressing for work. Another man joins them in bed, and we found it a real turn-on to hear lovers out of breath and see them clumsy with anticipation.

The last scene isn't particularly good. Although I found the woman sort of sexy, reminding me of Jeanna Fine, with short dark hair and a nice body, Beth thought the two men were very unattractive. I had to agree. I gave them points for orgasming twice each but I'd watch the first two scenes and just skip the last. This was the first amateur video we watched, and despite the final scene, enjoyable.

HEAD OVER HEELS

This one starts off with a nice long scene of a woman shaving another woman's vagina. This first scene takes a while, but it is fun to watch, especially when they proceed to sex toys. A second scene, when the two women are joined by a man, didn't do much for either of us, but a final scene of a husband and wife was arousing, as the couple are obviously in love with each other. Also, the scene seems more like a video the couple themselves use for stimulation. The husband employs the camera, but is still a part of the action. I like amateur videos better when the participants at the very least acknowledge the presence of a cameraman. This scene, though, like many amateur efforts, could benefit from tighter editing. We got a little nauseated during some of the camera position transitions.

ASHLEY & MARIA

This is another first-person perspective video, though this time the male lensman never joins in, save for a hand from behind the camera. He interviews the woman as if they're strangers, but it's obvious they're a couple and this is filmed in their home. The erotic dialogue between them is quite sexy, and the tape is intended to be seen by a couples audience. Ashley's first sex scene begins with manual masturbation, proceeds to sex toys, and ends with an intense orgasm, which actually occurs off-camera. I guess someone wanted his hands free. Besides, she quickly has another one, so who can complain? The action switches to Maria, who is also interviewed before she begins caressing herself, then is joined by Ashley. Though she's talked a good bisexual game thus far, it's clear she's a novice. It's also damn clear she enjoys it, and she enthusiastically returns the favor. Though the video lacks a male lead, *Ashley & Maria* offers some very steamy couples-oriented sex.

Video Alternatives is a solid company that offers a high-quality bang for the buck. If realistic sex between next-door-neighbor types excites you, these videos from their catalog will please you immensely.

Glossary

Toss some of these terms around at your next cocktail party and you're sure to grab some attention.

Auto-fellatio—The rare ability for a male performer to give himself oral sex. The chief practitioner of this stunt is the legendary Ron Jeremy. Can be seen, briefly, doing so in *The Devil in Miss Jones II*. Sadly, he's now too rotund to perform this feat admirably.

Breaking down on the set—Male performer losing his erection during a scene.

Cowgirl—Woman on top of recumbent man, each facing each other. As in "Ride 'em, cowgirl." (See Reverse Cowgirl.)

DP—Double penetration. Two male performers, one female, penises in vagina and anus.

DAP—Double anal penetration. Two penises in anus.

DPP—Double pussy penetration. Two penises in vagina.

Facial—Ejaculation delivered to the face. Standard in most videos today.

Fill-in girls—Low-level talent who will probably never reach star level.

Fisting—An entire hand in a vagina or anus (in a gay video). Not usually seen in modern tapes as it is now considered obscene.

Fluff girls—Also known as Fluffers. Women who keep the male actors aroused between takes.

Golden shower—One performer urinating on another. Now considered obscene.

Money shot (Pop shot, Cum shot)—Ejaculation.

Raincoater—The type of guy who goes to porn theaters and masturbates while watching the film.

Reverse cowgirl—The same as cowgirl, only the woman is facing the man's feet.

RCA—Reverse cowgirl with anal-Same as above with anal penetration.

RCDP—Reverse cowgirl with double penetration.

Sixty-nine—Two performers having oral sex with each other, head to toe.

Spooning—Female and male lying side by side, man behind.

Squirting—Female ejaculation.

Stunt dick—Bringing in another male to use in close-up scenes when the main actor is unable to remain erect or produce the money shot.

Suitcase pimps—Some of the particularly obnoxious boyfriends or husbands of female stars who consider themselves indispensable agents and managers.

Top—The half of a gay sex scene who is literally on top. The dominant male.

TP—Triple penetration. Penis in mouth, anus, and vagina.

Waiting for wood—Doesn't this have a wonderful ring to it? This means the time period where cast and crew stand around waiting for the male performer to get hard enough to get into the scene.

Wall to waller—Tape that is all sex, no story.

Afterword
You're On Your Own

By now you should know what we like, and if you've tried out any of these movies you should know what you like. It's time you spread your wings and learned to fly on your own. With more than five thousand erotic videos produced each year, you have plenty to pick from.

We hope you enjoyed this book, and we'd love to hear what you think about it and about erotic videos in general. Write to us via our publisher, St. Martin's Press, 175 Fifth Avenue, New York, N.Y., 10010. Those of you with computers and modems can look for us on the World Wide Web where we hope to have a Web page.

Remember, life is to be enjoyed—find pleasure, and love, in one another.

Steve and Beth Brent
Long Island, New York

Index

Craig, Ted, 122
Cramer, Nic, 131
Crichton, Michael, 106
Crosby, Denise, 76
Cross, Carol, 82–83, 88
Cummings, Dave, 102
Cynthia and the Pocket Rocket,
  134–35

Daisy, 135, 139
Dallas, 102, 123, 133, 143
D'Amato, Joe, 143, 146
Damiano, Gerard, 99, 100
Danell, Capri, 109
Daniels, Evan, 133
Daniels, Ian, 136
Dark, Gregory, 38, 101, 102
Dark brothers, *50*
Darrian, Racquel, 116, 124–26,
  164
Dave, Slave, 171–72
Davis, Mark, *44,* 102, 119, 122,
  135, 139, 143
Day, Ariel, 156–57
Debbie Does Dallas, 99–100
De Brun, Marc, 114
Debutante series, *177–78,* 182
Deep Throat, 14
Deloin, Alain, 179
Del Rio, Vanessa, 103
Deshaffer, Christine, 103
DeSilva, Guy, 133
Desire, 46, 50, *109–10*
Devil in Miss Jones, The, 99, *100*
Devil in Miss Jones II, The, 45, 99,
  100–101, 189
Devil in Miss Jones III and IV, The,
  101–2
Devil in Miss Jones 5: The Inferno
  (DMJ5), 38, 39, 44, 50, *102–3*
De Vries, Tanja, 114
Dial, Nikki, 124, 170–71
Diamond, Debi, 119, 135–36, 144,
  150–51, 159–61

Dinner Party, The, 44, 45, 51,
  135–36
Dirty Western II, 136–37
Diva, 159, 160
Divine, 123
Doda, 174
Dodger, Rodger T., 85
Dodson, Betty, 88, *95–96*
Dog Walker, 45, 46, 51, *137–38*
Dol, Veronica, 111
Doll, Barbara, 102, 147, 164
Don Juan DeMarco, 55
Double Dare, 76–79
Dough, Jon, *44,* 109–10, 116, 122,
  129–31, 137–38, 147, 159–61,
  167–68, 170
Douglas, Michael, 11
Dracula Exotica, 103
Draghixa, 139, 153
Drake, Steve, 110, 120, 133, 140–
  41, 150, 154, 160–61, 164
Duchovny, David, *73–74,* 76, 79,
  80
Dulany, Caitlin, 79
Dunn, John, 117
Dunning, Judd, 89–90
Duvall, Robert, 133

E., Nick, 124, 129
East, Nick, *44,* 102, 131, 133, 135,
  151, 155–56
Eastern, Jessie, 168
Edwards, Eric, 99, 103, 107
Ekberg, Marita, 82
Elements of Desire, 39, 51, *139*
Elodie, 153
Emerson, Wesley, 161
English, Toni, 150
Enjoying Sex, 96–97
Enright, Jim, 134
Erotica West, 181
Erotika, 44, 51, *139–40*
Estrada, Emerald, 147
Evans, Warren, 103